Intergroup and Minority Relations:
An Experiential Handbook

Edited by

Howard L. Fromkin
Purdue University
John J. Sherwood
Purdue University

UNIVERSITY ASSOCIATES, INC.
7596 Eads Avenue
La Jolla, California 92037

Contents

Intergroup Awareness and Communication

Fantasies

Role Playing and Role Reversals

STRUCTURED EXPERIENCES: INTERGROUP

Introduction

Experience-Based Learning and Intergroup Contacts

The decade of the 1960s will be recorded by social historians as the time when minorities in American society stood up and demanded two things —acceptance of their individuality as people and equal rights as citizens. The voices and actions of blacks who were no longer willing to settle for less began the fractionization. American Indians have continued the movement by calling attention to their heritage by encircling a city, a prison, and a monastery. Migrant workers have utilized the boycott as an effective weapon against a powerful majority. Women have demanded to be identified as people of competence who are capable of choice. The poor demand to be heard by the affluent. The day that people can, with conscience, treat others as "niggers"—whether they be students, women, blacks, or others—has passed.

Our constitution and legislation requiring equal employment opportunities are formal forces toward affirmative action. Furthermore, this society cannot progress without the talents, skills, resources, and perspectives of those who are "different." We no longer can allow groups of people to live side by side in hatred, servitude, or exploitation.

This book is intended to assist persons in working effectively with groups of "different" people. It reports some creative efforts and procedures to help members of different groups expand their perspectives of themselves and of other persons and explore more fully their choices for action. While the book's focus is often on blacks, both because of their visibility and their leadership during recent years, its intention is much broader. The contents of this book can be easily modified to improve relations between people and groups who are different from one another in terms of age, race, sex, occupation, and the roles and norms associated with these generic categories.

1

The specific experiments, experiences, and activities contained in this volume are designed to increase a person's understanding of some of the essential characteristics of persistent conflict between groups: ethnocentrism (self-assumed superiority of one's own perspectives, values, and actions); the misplacement of one's own problems onto others as if they arose from the other group's inadequacies; denial of access to desired resources or opportunities; and disproportionate distribution of power. However, we recognize that racism, sexism, and other forms of denigrating the values of others to our own advantage are *not simply* matters of individuals' stereotyping, prejudice, and bigotry. While these factors are important, we also recognize that the balance of power in society must be altered in some fundamental ways before certain minority groups can successfully control their own fate.

DESIGN OF THE BOOK

The book is organized into four major sections: workshop designs, structured experiences, instrumentation, and resources. The design section contains nine descriptions of experience-based programs with a variety of objectives, such as increasing interracial empathy, trust, understanding, and communication, and building human relations skills in the context of affirmative action or community problem-solving workshops. The participants vary from academics to community leaders to industrial managers, and the settings are just as varied. Program descriptions are included in this section because they provide examples of how a variety of activities can be integrated to meet specific objectives. Many of the designs provide helpful suggestions for planning and implementing interracial workshops.

This collection of materials is neither comprehensive nor exhaustive; it is meant to be simply a varied and provocative survey. No general principles of design for intergroup awareness and change are presented, because we do not believe that a set of general principles exists. Instead, we offer anecdotal stimuli to help in the selection of experiences for the design of intergroup or interracial learning and exploration. The designs allow us to learn from the experiences of others by observing their successes or near successes.

Each of the descriptions has a special strength to offer. For instance, Don Dawson offers a workshop for whites to expand awareness of white racism and to initiate anti-racism action outcomes. Jane Moosbruker and Dean Holt recommend an innovative use of the Thematic Apperception Test, which was developed for other purposes in basic motivational research. John Denham and Maxine Thornton-Denham describe a weekend training workshop that was designed for a group of people who wanted to understand their own racism in order to work more effectively to combat racism in their community. Ruth King describes a multi-media approach using popular music and poetry to build positive identification among black youth. James Richard's paper delineates a collaborative effort by community leaders, local business people, and the faculty of a business school to train a cadre of consultants in interracial problem solving; the aim was to improve minority employment programs in local businesses. Cyril Mill highlights the importance of goal setting as a necessary preliminary step in the design of intergroup experiences. Donald Goldman and Eugene Cincotta describe the need for a planning meeting with potential participants prior to beginning the actual program. Arthur Freedman outlines a program that increased interracial communication and trust—and, at the same time, produced some tangible plans to implement potential solutions to interracial problems in the community. Similarly, Thomas Woodall provides an example of a ghetto workshop that integrated exercises with attempts to find solutions for real community problems.

Most of the authors also describe their perceptions of the effects of the interracial training activities on the participants and the community. Although these observations are in the form of anecdotal reports and are not intended as thorough and systematic evaluations, they are reported by experienced professionals and may be helpful to others in the design of future intergroup experiences. With the experiences of others before us, we can set more realistic expectations regarding potential outcomes.

The section on structured experiences contains nineteen activities that are, in general, intended to expand the participants' awareness of their own ideas and behavior, the effect these have on other people, and the way in which their own ideas and behavior can facilitate or block the achievement of their personal or group objectives. It is assumed that awareness is one component of improving communication between groups and that it is a necessary, but not a sufficient, condition for intergroup cooperation.

A variety of more specific objectives can also be found among the structured experiences. Each of the activities contains its particular statement of objectives. Somewhat arbitrarily, we have classified the structured experiences under two major headings: (1) personal and interpersonal (comprising the subdivisions of getting acquainted and warm-up, intergroup awareness and communication, fantasies, and role playing and role reversals); and (2) intergroup (including the topics of competition, power and cooperation). Yet any activity is easily modified to suit a multitude of objectives and to fit a wide variety of programs.

The section on instrumentation contains four paper-and-pencil devices useful in both training and evaluation. The classic "Chitlin' Test" is followed by a unique projective test—"Three Photos." An attitude inventory is included, and the section is completed by a survey of opinions about equal employment opportunity.

Finally, the section on resources contains references, films, tapes, and training packages that can be used as supplemental materials in intergroup and minority workshops. A list of individual contributors' names and addresses concludes the book.

Workshop Designs

Anti-Racism Training:
A One-Day Workshop on White Racism

DON M. DAWSON

BACKGROUND

In the fall of 1972, a state interreligious commission on human equality decided to take a critical look at its present programs and the directions it wished to take in the future. Most of the commission board members were white, and they were convinced that the issue and reality of personal and institutional racism must be dealt with throughout the state. As a result of this conviction, an anti-racism training program was established.[1] Since March, 1973, this program has sponsored twenty-five workshops with religious and educational groups in the state, using the model of anti-racism training described in this paper.

Staff

Staff teams are composed of three to five members, with a majority of whites and at least one black. The emphasis on white team members stresses the need for whites to work with each other on a white problem. Staff members have skills in group dynamics and have previously participated in anti-racism workshops. Other individuals with particular expertise in these areas also serve as team members, depending on the make-up of the participant group.

---

[1]DART (Development of Anti-Racism Training), a program of the Indiana Interreligious Commission on Human Equality.

Participants

Although the anti-racism workshop is designed for whites, some black participation is helpful. Twenty to twenty-five persons is the ideal group size, in order to allow for a variety of life experiences and to have maximum time for each person to participate. The group may be composed of strangers who have come together to consider racism, or it may be a task group that has an ongoing relationship.

GOALS

The main goal of the anti-racism workshop is to make the white participants aware of personal and institutional racism and for them to "own" responsibility for its existence.

The rationale behind this workshop is that there is only white racism in the United States and that the reactions of blacks to this white racism cannot be called black racism. Racism is defined as follows: "Racism, as it operates in the United States, exists when the majority population uses the power of its economic, social, educational, political, and religious institutions to suppress and discriminate against the minority population." In this definition, the "majority population" is clearly the white population.

A secondary goal of the workshop is to help the participants, individually or as a group, design action plans to combat racism.

DESIGN

There are a variety of components from which each workshop is constructed. Listed below is one model that has been used.

1. The following ground rules are established:
   a. The day is centered on black-white issues and is not to be side-tracked into other minority-group issues.
   b. Everyone must speak for himself, use "I" whenever possible, and avoid using "we," "us," and "the group."
   c. Although history will be dealt with as black-white issues are considered, participants are encouraged to deal with their current feelings and thoughts—to keep their remarks in the here-and-now.
   d. Openness and honesty are encouraged, and conflict is not avoided.
   e. Everyone is responsible for his own participation and for enforcing these norms.

2. A getting-acquainted session is held (when necessary) along with an assessment of present feelings about black-white issues.
   a. Each participant is asked to complete this sentence on a card: "America's race problem is . . ." (These cards are used later in the day to solicit the participants' reactions.)
   b. Each participant is asked to relate his earliest and most recent remembrance of "race." (Team members respond to these comments, centering on particular comments that identify the black-white issue as a black problem.)

3. Participants read articles from the *Black Chronicle* (developed and produced by Blackside Inc. for Holt, Rinehart and Winston, Inc., © 1971, Blackside Inc., Boston, Massachusetts) or a similar black periodical, and listen to tapes by Malcolm X and by a Ku Klux Klan speaker, to underline the treatment of blacks by whites from the past to the present. The participants then respond on a card by completing the statement "I feel (angry, hurt, neutral, sad, guilty, etc.) because I . . ." (stating why they feel as they do).

   The team members and participants respond to the statements on the cards, confronting those who are not dealing personally with the black-white issue.

4. A lecturette is given, dealing with a model of white society that controls the power, operating assumptions (value system), policies and norms of institutions, and benefits that are enjoyed primarily by the white society. A handout, "The New White Person" (see the end of this design), is distributed, describing how whites must deal with racism if there is to be change in black-white problem areas. In small groups, Terry's points on "The New White Person" are discussed.

   At this point in the day, it is hoped that most participants have recognized their own contributions and responsibilities in black-white issues and have named racism as basically a white problem.

5. If some people still feel strongly that both black racism and white racism exist, it is helpful at this point to list the results and effects of so-called black racism against whites, then of white racism against blacks, and to compare the differences.

6. The following circle activity is conducted to demonstrate how white racism operates in institutions. It is designed to show how whites become programmed to keep blacks out of their groups, how blacks who do get through can "become" white, and how

blacks who repeatedly cannot get through turn to separation (e.g., "We'll make it on our own without whitey"). In this manner, it is hoped that whites will see the underlying racist practices behind such alienation.

a. Eight to ten people, including at least one black participant, are asked to form a circle. One white person is asked to leave the room and, when he returns, to try to break into the circle. When the white person has left the room, the group is told to keep him out of the circle by whatever means are necessary.

b. After the white person has attempted to break into the circle, then others (both black and white persons) are asked individually to break into the circle.

c. Finally, a black team member is asked to break into the circle. However, he is instructed privately to walk around the circle and then to leave the room without attempting to break in.

d. The circle members sit down, and the following questions are asked:

(1) Why did you keep everyone out, when you were told only to keep the first person out?

(2) How did you feel when you kept the people out?

(3) How did you (black member) feel about keeping other blacks out?

(4) What was your reaction to the black team member who left the room without trying to break into the circle? Did you want to go after him? (The black team member who left represents black separation.)

7. Participants are asked, "What can you do personally and/or as a group about what you have experienced today?"

a. Participants list on a chalkboard or on newsprint several actions they can take.

b. Out of these, one to three actions are selected that can be accomplished soon with the least roadblocks. (Participants should consider if they have the power, money, time, commitment, etc., to do it.)

c. The participants set dates and name individuals who will be responsible to accomplish these action plans against white racism.

8. In an evaluation and follow-up discussion, each participant is asked to write at least three positive and three negative reactions to the workshop experience. These evaluations are studied by the staff team members, with reference to future workshops.

The team leader establishes a given date with a representative of the participants in order to see what progress has been made on the action plans and to offer assistance.

The New White Person

Some of us whites are experiencing a new consciousness of our whiteness and feel the urge to push this awareness to its limits. Awaking to the truth of our minority status among world populations, we want to ask if our whiteness can stand for anything positive, and, if so, what actions are required of us to deal humanely with the realities that confront us. If as White Persons we seek integrity for ourselves and justice for everyone, what does the new scene require of us? Here we propose some sketchings of The New White Person.

(1) THE NEW WHITE PERSON MOVES BEYOND GUILT to reality-action aimed at justice. Acknowledging our own racism and that of society, we must mobilize for change, not out of guilt for the past, but out of commitment to the future. We need not waste time with self-incrimination or verbal abuse from others; rather, let us move deliberately to discover and deal with real causes and solutions.

Not forgetting the shame of our history, we can nevertheless undertake to recover a sense of integrity for ourselves and a fair share of the "pie" for others, for we understand that psychic wholeness for whites and political/economic power for blacks are both critically urgent goals that cannot be independently achieved.

(2) THE NEW WHITE PERSON VALUES SELF WORTH. Paralleling the new consciousness of others, we will value ourselves as people and celebrate our beauty. We will consider ourselves important, even before we act. Therefore, we need not undertake projects to prove our worth. We will accept ourselves and act out of that security. We will no longer need to search for that liberal "good feeling."

Understanding black rage, but not intimidated by black power, we will move out of our own strength to support black empowerment.

(3) THE NEW WHITE PERSON UNDERSTANDS POWER and the ways of dealing with those in power. If justice is to prevail, changing attitudes is not enough. Powers that determine the present must be modified or replaced by powers that will shape tomorrow.

The idea of "white power" is for most whites a lifelong illusion, for in American society real power is held only by a very few men, corporations, and institutions. Most white people, too, are victims, not oppressors, used by those in power to maintain a racist system that locks everyone in. The future of The New White Person is not tied to the super-rich, but to those who take more responsibility for their own lives.

Adapted from Robert W. Terry, *For Whites Only,* Grand Rapids, Mich.: Eerdsmans, 1970, by the Center for Social Change (Paul J. Schulze, Director), 3137 Telegraph Avenue, Oakland, California 94609.

(4)   THE NEW WHITE PERSON IS A PRO-ACTOR, NOT A RE-ACTOR. We are ready to initiate change, not merely to respond to bad results. We know that change will not come unless political initiative can be wrested from those committed to preserving the status quo. We will be political beings who select allies and form coalitions that can effectively challenge the powers that be.

(5)   THE NEW WHITE PERSON ACCEPTS "SELF-INTEREST" as a valid notion for everyone to live by. We move to the understanding that self-interest is not the same as selfishness. We know that on a crowded planet shrinking in size, the survival of others is linked to our own and that we will be allowed no sleep if others are allowed no food.

This does not mean that New White Persons will be "pals" with every-one; but neither will we be patron or pawn. When self-interests clash and conflict emerges, ground rules must be negotiated, or none will survive.

On the international scene, we recognize that it will be to the realistic self-interest of whites to learn to play an appropriate and creative role as a minority race among the colored majority, not in order to ingeniously maintain control, but to enjoy dignity in peace with other peoples who are taking power commensurate with their numbers.

(6)   THE NEW WHITE PERSON TAKES RISKS. If we act for change, we must expect retaliation from those who oppose us. And if our wallet is the point at which we are most vulnerable, we may need to move toward a less expensive living standard. When we no longer require the "sweet pastries" of abundance and are willing to earn only "bread," we become free to release new energies for shaping a new society.

(7)   THE NEW WHITE PERSON IS OPEN TO NEW LIFE STYLES and sees the connection between life style and life commitment. This means we will explore new concepts of vocation and leisure, of land use, of women's rights, of education, and of "family," for all these will flow into the picture of what will be tomorrow's more open world.

(8)   THE NEW WHITE PERSON IS COMMITTED TO PLURALISM. We appreciate many cultures, many groups, many persons different from ourselves. But we do not feel compelled to imitate them or demand that they be like us. Willing to live in conflict and able to endure ambiguity, as New Whites we will celebrate the many diverse capabilities and tensions within ourselves, and delight in the rich potentials of other persons and cultures. Going beyond Voltaire's promise to defend another's right to "say," as New White Persons we will defend the other's right to "be."

(9)   THE NEW WHITE PERSON NEEDS SUPPORT GROUPS to provide the security that will encourage openness and growth. We recognize the need for kindred spirits to support our egos, maintain our sense of security, and stimulate our move into new consciousness. Support groups would provide opportunities for evaluating, strategizing, and

celebrating. They would be places for honesty and love, criticism and forgiveness.

Be they churches or communes, large or small, these support systems need to be cultivated in a deliberate and conscious manner. If a non-alienating society is to become a reality, people must be in touch with themselves, and practice at first hand how to live with, be sensitive to, and respect the moods, words, and values of others. From such learning/sharing communities, people can draw strength and wisdom and forge a world community in which all people can live humanely.

Workshop on White Racism

JANE MOOSBRUKER
DEAN A. HOLT

BACKGROUND

A great many efforts in recent years have been directed toward building multi-racial training and learning groups designed to explore racial tensions. Most of these groups have reached out toward some sort of confrontation between members of different races, with a negotiated settlement afterward. But a multi-racial confrontation group cannot really touch the problem at its source. White racism is a white problem, and the only people who can deal with it directly are whites. Black people do not know what it feels like; they recognize it only by its effect on them.

The majority of whites do not identify cultural racism as part of their own perspective. They see it as someone else's problem. But one is a racist in the sense that he sees and responds to black people differently than he responds to white people, or he has certain feelings and/or stereotypes about blacks that he does not have about whites.

A training design focusing on white racism can afford people the opportunity to see themselves in light of their feelings about people who are different from themselves. The revelation can be profoundly moving. The basic premise is that prejudice is, by definition, irrational. When irrational beliefs are fully examined so that their roots are found, they can be shown to be irrational. If enough help and encouragement are offered, the prejudice can be replaced by knowledge and understanding.

Staff

Two trainers, one male and one female.

Participants

An all-white group with a maximum of twenty participants.

GOALS

A recognition of the feelings that make up racism can be achieved through a training experience. The training is not meant to scold or berate, only to provide a consciously supportive and authentic atmosphere in which real feelings can be accurately and completely explored. An experiential learning approach can focus on the interactions of participants, encouraging a climate of trust and openness, self-discovery, feedback, and the exploration of personal perceptions and reactions.

DESIGN

The lab design can achieve effective results in as short a period of time as a day and a half, by initiating a longer-lasting growth and change process in individuals. It can also be extended, if desired, to two or three days.

The basic design is to show pictures of black children, black men and women, and blacks and whites together. Each picture is used as a separate stimulus to which group members react and then share their feelings and associations with one another.[1] The pictures are carefully selected for their complexity and ambiguity, so that they draw very different reactions from different people. They are also ordered in a graduating degree of "threat value," i.e., with a brown-skinned Charlie Brown appearing first and an interracial sexual situation appearing last.

At first, only differences in the way the pictures are perceived are discussed by the group. This alone warrants much exploration and can stimulate an awareness of stereotypes or insensitivity to the differences between black and white cultures. As the group-building process continues, there is more trust and more sharing of emotional reactions to the pictures. Some of these feelings include distaste and fear. Because of the focus on self-awareness and awareness of others in the group, and because blacks are present, after all, only in pictures, members are more

---

[1]The theory explaining the effectiveness of this approach (association to ambiguous pictures) can be found in H. A. Murray's *Thematic Apperception Test,* Harvard University Press, Cambridge, Massachusetts, 1943.

likely to recognize their own negative feelings as prejudices. In other words, *they do not have to be told if they are prejudiced—they discover it.*

At this point, a process of discovery has begun. Each person is free to share his feelings with the group, to attempt to get help, or merely to sit and think. Once an expansion of self-awareness has occurred, a growth process has begun and is likely to continue.

In addition to the basic design, there are other possible inputs that can be used with different groups at the trainer's option. The most important is music, which is used in the same manner as the pictures, i.e., as a stimulus to which individuals react. Music that comes out of black culture can provide a more powerful "black presence" than pictures and can reach some people who are having difficulty reacting to the pictures. The selections are chosen on the basis of words, artist, and beat. When chosen primarily for the beat, black music can provide people with an opportunity to explore their feelings while moving to the rhythm.

Another option is the use of a simulated society game with an unequal distribution of wealth and power. The game is sufficiently involving that people begin to play roles of the wealthy and powerful and roles of the poor and apathetic. They then have an opportunity to look at and to discuss their own behavior, e.g., how easy it is to be influenced by one's own situation and not be aware of the other person's situation.

In summary, the workshop is a short, intensive, and profound exploration of one's own feelings and attitudes about those of different races. The learning method is that of self-discovery stimulated by cross-racial pictures and music. Participants have the opportunity to achieve a clear view of their own feelings and perceptions and to discuss what effects these feelings and perceptions can have on their everyday behavior.

Racism as Game and Reality

JOHN DENHAM
MAXINE THORNTON-DENHAM

Recently an innovative use of the laboratory approach was tried in an all-white bedroom community near New York City with a reputation for being a white refuge.

A small number of "white liberals" had joined with blacks from surrounding communities to take part in the struggles of blacks in the urban area. They created an organization named "Operation Understanding" whose goal was to promote racial understanding in the community. They realized that they themselves were not exempt from racist attitudes. The writers were called in to provide a weekend of training to help them deal with their own racism so that they could work more effectively to combat racism in their community. The laboratory was nonresidential, about 15 per cent black, and used a church parish hall for meeting.

Unfreezing and Warming Up

The design began with three experiential verbal and nonverbal sequences. The first was a milling exercise in six stages. Its purpose was to enable participants to experience their own similarities to and differences from others. It also provided some brief verbal expression of concerns about the black/white issue.

The second sequence emphasized selective recall of interracial experience and fantasy work with other participants.

Reprinted from *Human Relations Training News*, Vol. 14, No. 2, 1970, NTL Institute for Applied Behavioral Science, Arlington, Virginia. Reprinted by permission of the publisher and the authors.

The third sequence worked at surfacing fears and hopes in the small work group setting and legitimatizing these fears and hopes by asking participants to literally wear them on papers pinned to their clothing.

Within each sequence there was provided time for verbal reflection with several others. The effect of this work was to sanction and reward increased openness and honesty and to expose widely varying interracial experience as legitimate data for learning.

After an evening of unfreezing exercises focused on black/white issues, the purposes of the weekend were stated again to the whole group. It was emphasized that the laboratory would not deal with action planning or what to do about white racism. Instead it would deal with whatever dynamics were raised in the here-and-now experience of those present: how we felt, what we did, what interaction took place.

The Yellow/Green Game

The primary design feature of the weekend was then introduced. A length of green or yellow crepe paper was given to each participant and staff member. One of the staff members gave the following instructions:

"Green people in this community have been thought of as superior, capable, moral, able and intelligent. Yellow people are thought of as not quite as superior, not quite as capable, somewhat less moral and not as able. It has always been that way in this community. It has also been a custom that the green people occupy the first floor of this building, with its carpeted lounge, whereas the yellow people occupy the basement where the furnace is.

"You may negotiate to exchange your sash with anyone. The exchange must be agreeable to you both. [Time was given to do this.]

"You may not feel superior or inferior, but the sash indicates what others of your color have thought or felt about themselves. Allow yourself to 'get into' the color. Identify with it. Be yourself in this color. Feel your own feelings in it. React as you would react within the givens of your color.

"This culture will exist for the next three hours. The staff will fully participate in it. Let's begin."

The greens began to congregate in the lounge with its comfortable furniture and rug. Most of the yellows began to collect with each other and move toward the basement with statements such as, "Let's get out of here; I feel uncomfortable already."

In the basement, the yellows began to make attempts to develop a culture of their own. Gradually the yellows began to show many of the characteristics of a minority group, even though their number was equal to the greens. Several yellows left the basement room to steal cake from the first floor kitchen. Others went upstairs to get phonograph records.

Others simply went up to look at the greens and see what they were like. Some wandering yellows found an unused room on the first floor. All other yellows then moved up to the first floor and started to "caucus" in that room.

The pressure began to mount and the yellows felt frustrated, disintegrated and unable to accomplish anything through planning.

Several greens knocked on the door and asked to be admitted to make an appeal. Permission was refused. One green returned with another appeal. So great was the feeling against her intrusion that she was bodily removed from the room.

Meanwhile the greens met in the carpeted lounge with some yellow visitors present. Green attitudes included a "conservative right wing" point of view, "green liberals," and some who "didn't know where they stood." Soon the green conservatives and the green liberals left the room.

The green liberals took with them the remaining yellow visitors. They met and discussed how to make the portion of the first floor they occupied an "integrated neighborhood," and later, the idea of a commune was worked on.

The conservative green group met and discussed how it could maintain the green integrity of the first floor. Members of that group ranged in feeling from those who felt the whole issue was unimportant to those who were intent on not giving an inch to the yellows.

A third group of "I don't know where I stand" people met apart to share their feeling about the whole experiment. There was a clear "I don't want to be involved in this mess" attitude.

When two and one-half hours of the three-hour experience had elapsed, the yellow group was in a state of almost complete paralyzed frustration. During this period of much talk but no action frustration had reached the point where anything was acceptable in order to break the stalemate.

Even in this role play situation, inner tension and feelings of despair were quite real and demanded some sort of release. One of the men suggested a "paper riot." Spontaneously the yellows began to collect paper napkins, towels, toilet paper, trash, everything they could find. Then with great whoops and hollers and moans and groans they "invaded" the green area. The reactions of the greens were classic. The "I don't know" group withdrew to the sanctuary of the adjoining church building where they literally sat on the steps to the altar. They did not recognize what had happened as a "riot" but simply a fun and games effort to initiate fresh action.

The conservative greens remained where they were sitting, looking somewhat aghast and surprised, but did nothing. Someone from that group reported that the feeling present was one of becoming prepared in case such a thing should happen again. The liberal greens rose to their feet when the encounter had subsided and joined the yellows for soul music and dancing. Following the dancing the liberal greens and yellows were in many groups of two's and three's talking about what had happened and the feelings it had produced in them.

Following the experience, one hour was allowed for each of the original three small groups to meet, ventilate, and reflect on learnings from the morning. So painful had been the morning's activities that most of the participants could not "identify learnings." All they could discuss were their feelings, what had happened to them, how they reacted, and the emotions which were so present within them at that very moment.

The Yellow/Green Game Reversed

That afternoon it was announced that the experiment would be repeated with everyone reversing colors. There was loud resistance to this from most of the participants. The morning was too painful, they complained, but the staff announced that that was precisely why we were going to repeat the experience. Several participants got up to speak their approval. Reluctantly we started this all-too-real game once more. The dynamics could not have been more different. The greens did not fracture into the usual attitudinal divisions. Instead there were two groups discussing the issue with persons in each group playing the roles of arch-conservatives, liberals, and in-betweeners. On the side there were yellows and greens confronting each other, several of the yellows playing the roles of angry yellow militants with such vigor that the greens with them felt they were experiencing the real thing.

This experience was followed by an hour of ventilation and reflection. After dinner each person was encouraged to reflect alone for an hour on learnings from the day. The original three small groups then met at the end of the day to reflect on all that had taken place so far. There was much sharing of agony and the beginning of personal revelations relating to the black/white situation.

The next morning a film called "The Friendly Game" was shown and the three small groups met to share responses to it. This final session was very significant. Many persons who had withheld their private feelings throughout the weekend revealed them during this last time together. Some of the white liberals who had suffered much because of their positions shared their feelings. Others who had thought they were supportive admitted their new realization that their racism was still showing. Several of the blacks present confronted whites and the confrontation was returned. One of the groups with both blacks and whites came close to one another spontaneously standing with arms around shoulders, gently rocking and sharing thoughts with one another about what had happened.

Results of such a training experience are hard to evaluate. Only long term benefits ever measure the value of experiential learning. However, the written evaluations turned in by each person at the conclusion of the weekend indicated many personal insights into the meaning of the black/white struggle, white racism, and the emotions which lie behind many of the actions by black militants which so many whites find hard to understand.

Some Design Issues Defined

This training event involved some difficult training design issues that are worth commenting on. The first design issue involved breaking out of we/they compartmentalism: "We are liberal and okay; others in our town aren't." The design had to help the participants (both black and white) move from their "mental set" as well-informed, action-oriented, good-intentioned, concerned liberals to interaction with one another that brought to the surface authentic residual feelings of "whiteness" and "blackness." Our green/yellow game met this issue head on.

A second design problem involved working through "bad" feelings to "good" feelings. We trusted that a laboratory experience would expose prejudice, stereotyping, and subtleties of superiority-inferiority, but it would also trigger feelings of guilt, irrational anger, and coercive control within and between persons. As trainers, we had to help participants work through to "good feelings" of self-affirmation, strength, collaborative potential, and creative reality-testing with one another. The reversed second try of the game provided this opportunity and it continued in the Sunday morning reflection session.

A third design problem involved the client group's goal of better racial understanding. This was the initial and continuing basis of the group's being together. Individuals in the group had related goals interlaced with personal needs. The common ideological base needed a climate and setting wherein individuals could *meet* one another as fully as possible. We therefore tried to design a use of the laboratory method which would build such a climate, enable the level of commitment to the group goal to deepen, and provide the impetus for strengthening interpersonal support and trust. The combination of gaming plus the legitimatized intimacy of a small reflection group seemed to meet these design requirements.

Trainer Role Issues Defined

A participant-trainer stance seemed best. "Observer" or "consultant" or "detached trainer" models all seemed inappropriate in that they would make for distortion and parallel process problems. But a participant role held risk and promise related to the laboratory objective itself. We therefore tried to get in there with our own stuff of whiteness, blackness, personness, and also keep our skills and resources appropriately offered and flowing. Each of us became "a green" or "a yellow," sharing his own feelings openly and directly on behalf of himself *and* within the role reversal exercise while at the same time keeping the whole laboratory experience on target and in dynamic movement toward its conclusion.

Another issue for the trainers had to do with the variety and intensity of feelings and attitudes that might be triggered if the design really worked. Some of the participants were anxious people, or anxious about what was happening to them as they tried to work in Operation Understanding. Others were experiencing identity conflicts of a rather serious and painful nature. Still others were so well defended in their liberal point of view as "right" that the we/they syndrome seemed impenetrable and unshakable. Some were so action oriented that experiential learning might seem irrelevant and frustrating. One or two were so detached they might never "get in." We knew we had to be helpful and innovative with a wide range of attitudes.

Could we tune in accurately enough to individuals to know when and how to stroke, confront, emphasize, help expand norms, or put the lid on? We knew that it was important to know when and how to build, affirm, ignore inner conflicts, encourage health and growth, break through protective facades, support fraying egos, and encourage freedom of expression.

An interracial staff was a must. Each staff member needed to be in touch with his own feelings as a person as well as with his feelings about himself in the black/white struggle. Each staff member had to be strong enough to ride out any emergent feelings and associations in himself that might surface unexpectedly, perhaps previously unknown to him. We had to absorb into ourselves large amounts of anger and rage from others. We regard these factors very important in the selection of staffs for a black/white encounter of this kind.

Varied Applications

The basic confrontation game invented for this particular design has possible uses in a variety of other situations in which there is intergroup mistrust and misunderstanding, as with young people and "over-thirties."

Its usefulness lies in its combination of simulation and role reversal, an approach which not only enables the participant to see what it feels like to be in another's shoes, but also more of what it is to be in his own.

"I Am Somebody"
—Black Students' Self-Concept

RUTH G. KING

Success in school is related to self-esteem. And yet many self-concept studies have shown that black students, especially those of low socio-economic status, tend to hold lower concepts of self than white students; these black youth also tend to perform poorly in school (Frerichs, 1970; Ornstein, 1968).

The junior and senior high school counselor realizes that school is certainly one place where self-pride and confidence can be instilled in young people as an ongoing part of the educational process. Yet when he or she approaches the black student in the traditional counselor setting—on a one-to-one basis, the message that "black is beautiful" goes only skin deep. The outward signs of corn braids or Afro hairstyle, dashiki, or loyalty to soul sound almost cry out that black youth have not internalized the message of self-worth they must have to succeed. How could they? Within the context of a still hostile society, economic deprivation, lack of reinforcement of pride at home, many black youth come to school not ready to voice their aspirations or attempt serious study— not ready to be themselves or believe in themselves.

After some years in counseling black students, the author has developed a workshop, to be used primarily with black youths from ages 15-19, as a basis on which to build positive self-identification. Media such as popular music and poetry by black artists, the presentation of historical

Reprinted from *Social Change: Ideas & Applications,* Vol. 4, No. 1, 1974, NTL Institute for Applied Behavioral Science, Arlington, Virginia. Reprinted by permission of the publisher and the author.

fact to counteract myth, and pictures of famous and everyday black people are used to generate group and racial pride, which then stimulates personal feelings of pride and strength and beauty in every member.

The following model may be used by consultants, trainers, or teachers to stimulate positive feelings of self-worth in black youth. The mode is presented in three parts, each part taking approximately 2 hours.

WORKSHOP MODEL

Session I

Introduction

The purpose of getting together in this group today is to rap a while about black people. We want to think about ourselves as black people— what it really means to be black. We're going to rap a little while, then listen to some poetry and music and think about what they mean to us. Let's begin by listening to Marvin Gaye. Think about what he's really saying on the first cut, "What's Goin' On?"

Activity

Play record: "What's Goin' On?" Marvin Gaye—Tamla Records, TS310, side 1, cut 1.

Discussion Questions

(Music continues to play softly in background.)
  1. What's going on with black people today?
  2. Do black people need more love today?
  3. What do black people need to "make it" out there?
  4. (Summarize discussion when appropriate and lead into the next activity.) Now let's listen to what Rev. Jesse Jackson has to say about black people and what they need.

Activity

Play record: "I Am Somebody." Rev. Jesse Jackson—Respect Records, side 1, Tas 2601.

Discussion Questions

  1. In his sermon Rev. Jackson asked the question, "Who's holdin' you back?" He says that nobody's holding you back but yourself. Do you think that is so?
  2. Do you think black people put other blacks down? Why?

3. Let's think positive. How can black people be considered a strong race in this country?
4. Rev. Jesse said that both the black man and the black woman are strong. *What makes us strong? What makes us beautiful?*

Exercise—"I Am Somebody"

Listen to the first part of the record again. Then let's join the group in the record and repeat the words together to "I Am Somebody." (Record is played and group repeats words in unison.) Now each person in this group think of something that is strong and good in yourself. Let's use the words on the record, but change them a little. Say "I am somebody"; then in one sentence say something that is strong about yourself. *Example:* "I am somebody. I *have* a *will* of my own. I am somebody!" Let's go around the circle and repeat this as long as people want to say things about themselves.

Summary

How do you feel right now?

Was it hard to think of strong things in yourself? Was it hard to say them out loud? Why? Often it is easy to say negative things about ourselves or others, especially about others. Why do you think this is so? Often people think you are bragging if you talk positively about yourself. Everybody has strengths and if you want to make yourself better, you have to know what is strong in you, what is good in you, so you can work with it. Keep thinking about what is strong in you and what you've got going for you. See if you really know what those things are, and next time we will continue to work on finding our strengths.

Session II

Introduction

The last time we were together we listened to music by Marvin Gaye and a sermon by Rev. Jesse Jackson. We talked about how strong and beautiful black people are. The last thing we did was to say things about our own personal strengths. I asked you to think more about what YOU as a person have going for you. Let's get those thoughts together as we listen to Marvin Gaye again.

Activity

Play record: "What's Goin' On?" Marvin Gaye, side 1, cut 2.

Discussion

Before we get to the main question, let's think about what black people have going for them and take it all the way back to Africa.

1. Do you know of anything in our African culture that we still have going for us today?
2. There are some myths about black people that go back to Africa and right through the slavery period here. By myths, I mean that there are ways we had as part of our African culture that people in America didn't understand. They put the wrong meaning to what they saw, believed the wrong things, and in many cases still have us believing these wrong things, too. Do you know of any myths about black people? Why are they wrong? What is the correct meaning? How did things get so mixed up?
3. Let's talk about what each one of us has going for him or her right now.

Summary

Now that we have rapped about myths of black people and now that we understand the correct meanings, we can see what we have going for us much better.

Activity

Play record of poem "Ego Tripping" by Nikki Giovanni from the album "The Truth Is on Its Way"—Right-On Records, RR05001, side 1, cut 5.

Nikki Giovanni tells us how good she feels about herself in this poem. In fact, she went on a "trip," she felt so good. Let's listen to what she says when she is really feeling good about herself.

Discussion Questions

1. To do all the things Nikki talked about, you'd have to have a lot of power. What do you think you could do if you had lots of power?
2. What would you do for black people if you had the power?
3. What would you do for yourself?

Exercise—"Ego Tripping"

Let's go on our own ego trip as a group. Each person think of what he or she would do or give in the situation I describe. Imagine now that you have POWER! You're great! You are together! Each person repeat the first part of the sentence, then make up the last part yourself.

1. I was born in the Congo,
   I have a creative mind.
   One day I created _____.
2. I was born in the Congo,
   I have beautiful children.
   For his (her) birthday, I gave my son (daughter) _____.
3. I was born in the Congo,
   I am a strong person.
   With my strength I can _____.
4. I was born in the Congo,
   I am a beautiful person.
   I am so beautiful that _____.

Summary

That was really a cool trip. We ARE beautiful, strong black people! Next session we will continue to talk about what we can do as black people—what YOU can do with what you have as a beautiful black person.

Session III

Introduction

The last session we took a "trip" and imagined all the groovy things we could do if we had the power. Let's listen to the record "Outa-Space" and imagine yourself on the trip again. As you listen, make up things you could do and things others would do for you.

Activity

Play record "Outa-Space," by Billy Preston—A&M Records, #8558.
   1. Let's talk about some of the pictures that just went through your mind.
   2. Let's listen to the music again but this time let's move to the music.
      a. Move as if you have power.
      b. Move as if you have beauty.
      c. Move as if you are the most gentle, loving person.
      d. Move as if you can do anything you want to do.

Exercise—Fantasy

Sit on the floor or wherever you can relax and feel comfortable. Close your eyes and imagine you are the person you want to be. Nothing is holding you back . . . not even YOU. Just let your mind go . . . just imagine—

      a. Who are you?

      b. Where do you live?

      c. Do you have a family? Who is in it?

      d. What does your house or apartment look like?

      e. What is strong and beautiful about you?

      f. What can you do now that you can't do in real life?

Find one other person in the room that you like to rap with and share the thoughts you just had . . . Now let's share in the larger group.

Exercise—Identify

We've been talking about what we would do if nothing was holding us back. Here are some pictures of black people who are using what they have—their abilities and strengths—to do what they can for themselves and other people. Some are famous like Leon Sullivan, Ruby Dee, and Eldridge Cleaver. Some are just everyday folks like us. Look at the way they are dressed or see if something in the picture makes you feel close to that person. Walk around the room and find a picture of a person you really "dig" and think about the reason. Then share with the group the picture you like best and say what it means to you.

Exercise—Positive Bombardment

We have talked about the way we feel about the people in the pictures and what they mean to each of us. Now let's really take a look at each other. Choose a partner and sit by him. We've been talking all along about the strengths each of us has. Look at your partner and think about what is strong in your classmate. Take 5 minutes and talk to your partner about what you see that is strong in him or her. Partner listen, then tell the person how you can use the strength he sees in you. How can you make it work for yourself and make yourself better? (Change partners and repeat exercise two or three times.)

Closure

We've had a real time talking about black people and how we feel about ourselves. We are strong, we are beautiful! We just finished hearing someone tell us what is strong in each one of us. You talked about how to make this strength work for you. I'd like everyone to really try to do at least one of the things you said you could. You have the POWER. You can do what you want to do. If we want to stay strong as a people we have to keep doing this. When you leave today, keep thinking about strong things in yourself, keep doing what you can to make the strong things work for you. You got the power, baby.

Research Results and Adaptations

Ninety black students of low socioeconomic status in a large East Coast city who participated in a workshop of this design did improve their self-concept as measured by the Tennessee Self-Concept Scale and observations of behavior in the classroom over time. (The control group attended regular group counseling sessions while the experimental groups experienced the workshop.) The author suggests that follow-up mechanisms can easily be devised to assist youth in continuous self-assessment and personal growth.

The workshop model has been adapted to many training situations —even with enlisted men and officers in the U.S. Army—but its suggested uses are these:

- To facilitate an improved self-concept for black youth in conjunction with counseling techniques.
- To introduce a course or unit in black studies.
- As an ongoing process in the teaching of a black studies unit (or other units).
- To facilitate enhancement of self-concept of youth who are participants in special training programs or projects.

REFERENCES

Frerichs, A. H. Relationship of self-esteem of the disadvantaged to school success. *Journal of Negro Education,* 1970, *39,* 117–120.

Ornstein, A. C. The need for research on teaching the disadvantaged. *Journal of Negro Education,* 1968, *37,* 133–138.

Problems of Minority Employment

JAMES E. RICHARD

BACKGROUND

Much concern is expressed by industry about providing jobs and growth opportunities for underemployed and "unemployable" minority people. Efforts made by industry to open jobs to minorities and to create more opportunities for job placement and advancement often insufficiently address the magnitude of the problem. To assist in the implementation and progress of minority employment programs, an experimental seminar was conceived between an industrial human relations committee and a school of business administration. The seminar sought to cope with some of the problems that companies, individuals, and minority communities experience in the effort to provide more jobs and career opportunities for minority people.

Representatives from three local companies were invited to the planning discussion at the college. The three firms were committed to major efforts to employ and provide career opportunities for minorities. A college faculty was selected that could link the local community with the participating firms and provide experience from the college's school of business administration and psychology departments.

The faculty and company representatives wanted to address some of the barriers to genuine career advancement for minority people. They were especially concerned about backlash from stepped-up efforts to recruit, train, and advance black people. Prejudice on both sides, fear for job security among white employees, and insensitive low-trust relations were felt to be major barriers.

It was thought that no ordinary approach would do justice to the issues. The seminar was designed to initiate basic encounters among the

29

participants and the staff to penetrate superficial levels of experience and to build on the actual experience of the members—both black and white. The experimentation would seek to discover some conceptual schemes for dealing with these problems.

Staff

The seminar training staff was composed of six persons, each with especially pertinent experience: three black members with wide experience in the community and in other black communities, and three white members from the school of business administration and the psychology department, all with varied organizational experience. One person from the latter group took the central research responsibility, with a small group of graduate students assisting him.

Participants

Ten white persons from each participating company attended; they were about equally divided between first-line and higher-level management. In addition to these thirty participants, there was a special black training cadre of nine persons—three from each of the participating firms. These members held various jobs in the three firms, including skilled production operators, first-line supervisors, and staff members in training, labor relations, and purchasing.

GOALS

The objectives established for the experimental seminar were (1) to define the problems encountered by black employees, supervisors, the companies as organizations, and the black community in its efforts to advance community cohesion; (2) to work toward the resolution of problems; and (3) to develop follow-up programs as the companies indicated interest.

Specific program goals were (1) to train cadres of trainers within the companies in skills of interracial problem solving; (2) to train all other participants in skills of interracial problem solving; and (3) to provide support programs to reinforce the progress made by individuals once they have returned to their jobs.

DESIGN

Seven one-half-day seminar sessions were conducted on the college's campus on Friday mornings. The first was a training session in which only the staff and the black cadre met for team development of the cadre. The subsequent six meetings were various combinations of encounter meetings between the three basic groups of participants: management, foremen (first-line supervisors), and blacks. The staff was dispersed among the three groups.

The seminar was complex because:

1. It sought to simulate some of the structural relationships that cause conflict within the companies;
2. It sought to give expression to black employees' feelings and attitudes more intensely than they are expressed in normal daily encounters, but in such a way as to deal realistically with some of the deeper problems;
3. It sought to trace some of the key conflicts, both interracial and institutional, that obstruct individual and company career-development efforts.

A special effort was made to develop strong group cohesion within each of the three working groups. Special team-building sessions were held with each group for identification of common interests and to develop internal strength.

A second focus of the seminar design was to bring groups together to examine and deal with conflicting issues. In addition to the independent meetings of each group, the foremen met with the black cadre; the managers met with the black cadre; the managers met with the foremen; and, finally, the three groups met together in general sessions.

A third focus brought intra-company groups together—blacks, whites, foremen, and managers. By these means, various corporate structural problems were identified, which bear on interracial issues, but which also exist as corporate problems apart from majority-minority conflict.

Three difficulties were experienced with this procedure:

1. Some participants resisted the structuring, feeling that it created conflict artificially or unnecessarily and that insights would develop through more detached discussion.
2. The three company groups had different situations back home, and even though there was considerable value in intercompany exchange, there was also inhibition and traces of company rivalry.
3. The half-day sessions, once a week, were not long enough to deal adequately with the issues raised. (Sessions almost never ended at the scheduled times because of absorbing discussions.)

OUTCOMES

In spite of the difficulties, the seminar was a lively and productive series of work sessions. Within its broad objectives, the seminar identified such key problems as discrimination, whites' underrating of blacks, a need for better skills training, lack of foreman support, and the need for more interracial encounter training.

Of the more specific seminar goals, the staff believed that some significant training strategies were tested and verified. The staff concluded that the idea of a nucleus of black employees (the equivalent of an intra-company black cadre) and a nucleus of white advocate counterparts is sound. They felt that companies could sponsor programs for training trainers from within company ranks who, in turn, could work together to develop a gradually spreading network of informed company members.

The general approach proposed by the staff, based on the seminar experience and taken from supporting organization theory, was:

1. To utilize existing structures or create new structures to effect corporate education and attitude changes;
2. To train key trainers within departments or divisions to become the nucleus of the training network as an adjunct to their normal jobs;
3. To utilize existing line managers and operating people in this network of trainers as much as possible in conjunction with their regular jobs;
4. To define the role of this network as an influence and to advocate organization that works informally but does not have responsibility for decision making;
5. To expect this network to identify problems, facilitate communication, aid in the surfacing of issues, and train company employees in relationship skills through exposure, demonstrations, and direct contact experience;
6. To attain legitimization of the training and educational network by the top executive level.

Several significant concepts arose during the seminar. These were:

1. *Black people need group support when working in predominantly white organizations.* Individual blacks in large, white institutions are submerged and overwhelmed by the very weight of the white majority structure. Those who adapt often must change life-long habits, with a resultant loss of identity. They need support and reinforcement from other blacks to offset this loss. Consequently, it may be impossible for an individual minority person to main-

tain a sense of personal dignity if he is working alone in a majority setting.

2. *Black men are habitually underrated by white men in our society.* In many ways, white members of the seminar found themselves misunderstanding or underrating blacks. They were usually unaware of this until it was pointed out by the black cadre.

3. *The concept of individual treatment can be dysfunctional.* The widely held management tenet of individual treatment can work against white managers who are dealing with minority people. When a problem in communication or a lack of trust exists, as is often the case in interracial situations, the white manager may worsen the situation by dealing with black employees on an isolated, individual basis. Blacks interpret this as a "divide-and-conquer" tactic.

4. *Middle management (those above the foreman level but beneath the top) seemed to be the organizational level most involved in conflict.* This became the focal point of the seminar and generated the most difficult problems. While blacks and foremen quickly established rapport which moved toward cooperative and supportive relationships, the ambiguity of the middle managers' position became a barrier to problem solving. Middle managers appeared to have pressures on them that the foremen and black cadre were neither able to understand nor to deal with.

5. *First-line supervision needs some form of lateral (foreman-to-foreman) linking system in order to develop more upward influence in the organization.* All the weight of concrete, on-the-spot action converges at the first-line supervisory level, but the foreman is often so pressed for action that he lacks the perspective to implement new policy decisions of top management or to communicate his operating dilemmas upward.

6. *Company sanction should be given to some form of organizational black support structure (which would cooperate with the foreman support structure).* The force of top-down power, applied through managerial actions, often has the effect of pitting blacks against whites at lower levels in the organization, and of increasing pressure from both on the foremen. Upward influence from lower levels of organizations, officially sponsored by the company, can help reduce conflicts and can contribute valuable insight and vitality to company policies.

The seminar staff thought that further research was needed on such questions as:

1. What are the conditions affecting middle managers? What support measures might be taken to strengthen their position—in

the organization generally as well as relating specifically to the minority issue?

2. How can the company account for union (or employees' committee) interests? How might unions be brought into more constructive involvement?

3. How might top-level policy be linked better with some of the implementation problems of minority employment? Are time and cost dimensions realistically understood and accepted? Should efforts be made to influence governments to subsidize the margin of cost—which is a social cost—but necessary to success?

Recommendations

From the experience of this seminar, the staff recommended some alterations in design for future seminars and some additional company activities.

The following modifications in the design of future seminars were suggested:

1. Sessions should be longer in terms of consecutive hours on consecutive days—perhaps all-day meetings for three days.

2. Some company divisions need more internal work. Special divisional seminars dealing with policy, practice, and interpretation, which intermix employees from two or three levels, could be productive.

3. Specially designed middle-management and foremen groupings, with intergroup work between the two levels, are recommended.

4. There should be more intercompany planning to determine the amount and kinds of intercompany exchange required. There is potential value in such exchange, but details need to be worked out in advance.

The seminar staff concluded that every company has inherent resources for achieving constructive change in solving interracial problems in its internal environment.

This experimental effort in probing some of the basic problems of minority employment and career advancement was considered an important beginning.

Training the Hard-Core Unemployed

CYRIL R. MILL

BACKGROUND

Industry has encountered a number of difficulties associated with the recruitment and training of the hard-core unemployed for useful and productive work. These problems include proper assessment and job assignment of the trainee, problems in developing job attitudes and work skills to enable the trainee to adapt to work routines, and problems in building attitudes of acceptance among the existing work force. Because of these difficulties, a major corporation employed the laboratory training method to help alleviate some of the problems.

The corporation planned to recruit three hundred hard-core, unemployed blacks and Puerto Ricans during a year's time. They would be employed in groups of sixty per month, for five months. It was felt that if existing plant personnel were helped to relate to the newcomers, the trainees would be better able to survive the adjustment period.

The sponsoring corporation was not unionized. The closest thing to an inside, organized pressure group in the plant was the black brotherhood, who first interpreted the schooling of current personnel by management as brainwashing.

Initially, supervisors were asked to list human relations problems in the plant. There was a general denial of such problems at first, but as time went by, more and more issues—particularly black-white—began to surface. Because promotions seemed to go to those who did not "rock the boat," there was general resistance in the corporation to griping. Those who achieved promotion were usually those who maintained a positive attitude toward work and the work environment. Under this agreeable surface, however, feelings of dissatisfaction existed. There was a "young-versus-old" issue and a "Negro (Uncle Tom)-versus-militant-black" issue. This early data collection paved the way for direct confrontation among the participants in the main training that followed.

Staff

The training staff consisted of two black trainers from the NTL Institute. Members of the black brotherhood were invited to observe, and sometimes participate in, the training program.

Participants

Participants consisted of thirty-six supervisory personnel, two plant managers, and a number of trainees. About one-third were black.

GOALS

The purpose of the training was to help prepare personnel for the impending introduction of minority-group workers into the plant.

DESIGN

The lab began on a Monday morning and ran through Thursday afternoon. The sessions were held during working hours, with no night meetings. The program took place at a motel near the plant, an arrangement which helped take the participants away from the immediate pressures of their work and enabled them to eat and spend rest periods and breaks together in an informal way.

Monday morning began with an introduction of the staff and a brief explanation of the program. The rest of the morning was spent in a rap session, which was dominated by blacks. The blacks lectured the whites, receiving little rebuttal. At the end of the morning session, a question was put on the board for whites to answer: "Do you feel there really is a racist problem in this company?" All the whites answered affirmatively.

The afternoon began with a continuation of the bitter harangue by blacks against whites, revealing the blacks' underlying hostility. Several of the blacks expressed very low morale and talked openly about rioting, striking, and violent confrontations with the management as a means of drawing attention to their problems. An activity on collaboration was introduced to provide an alternative to this kind of behavior. The group formed quartets; each individual was to select a situation in which he would try to confront a peer, a subordinate, or a boss. Each participant was to state the situation and test the readiness for confrontation, to separate fact from fantasy, to state feelings, and to find a resolution. Each, in turn, was a confronter, a confrontee, and an observer. Nearly everyone participated in this activity.

Later in the afternoon, two T-groups were formed. Opportunities for direct feedback were found in these groups.

Tuesday morning began with a brief activity that enabled participants to talk with one another immediately. In as many cross-racial pairs as possible, their task was to find and list differences and similarities between racial groups. After about ten minutes, a count was listed on newsprint and, as predicted, more similarities were discovered than differences.

After this a listening activity, first modeled by the trainers, was developed. A brainstorm session of the total group revealed a list of relevant discussion topics. A typical sample topic was, "Should the corporation adopt a compensatory promotion plan for blacks?" Triads were formed (with one black and two whites) for the listening activity. Each person was to reflect on the meaning of the previous speaker, before speaking himself. Although this proved to be very difficult, the intimate climate was beneficial. Participants were divided into T-groups until lunch.

At lunch, half the group was asked to eat while wearing blindfolds. Because this activity had been discussed previously in the plant, there was no difficulty in implementing it. Blacks and whites seemed equally willing to be the dependent, blindfolded persons.

The blindfold activity was processed briefly after lunch and a theory session on the Johari Window was introduced. This was followed by quartet groupings in which participants practiced openness by telling each other something they would not ordinarily reveal to a new acquaintance, and by providing each other with feedback on their first impressions.

The remainder of the afternoon was spent in two T-groups with one group self-oriented and the other organizationally oriented. A member of the black brotherhood dominated one of the groups with another long lecture of injustices suffered by blacks. The question "What can whites do individually to reduce racism in the plant?" arose. The issue was brainstormed, and fifteen suggestions were posted on the board for the remainder of the lab. At the end of the afternoon, pairs from across the T-groups met in quartets to learn what was happening in the other T-group.

Since the concern about blacks resorting to violence was great, Wednesday morning began with a theory session on win-lose (the confrontation model), lose-lose (the riot model), and win-win (the collaboration model).

A competition-collaboration activity was then introduced. Each T-group was given the task of coming up with ten ideas that would go into a petition to the management to reduce racism in the plant. Next, each T-group was to elect three representatives to work with representatives of the other group in negotiating a final list of ten items. The choice of the topic caught the imagination of most of the participants. However, some of the black participants could not discriminate between this as a training task and as fact. Some of the whites were apparently intimidated, because they stood ready to withdraw from the workshop if the petition were actually sent to the management.

The selection of the ten items by each T-group took all Wednesday morning. One group brainstormed about fifty items from which it had to make a final selection of ten, a procedure that proved to be time-consuming. The other group was able to come up with only seven acceptable items, after which members suggested a few items not related to racism, such as a dental program for all employees. Both groups finally issued ten items for a petition.

Negotiations began in the afternoon, after a discussion of whether the training task was real or used merely for learning purposes. At this point many of the deep, "gut" reactions of the blacks came to the surface. They considered these issues very real, while they felt the whites were merely intellectualizing.

The negotiation session continued through the following morning before an agreement on the final ten items was reached. The trainers pointed out actual behaviors on the part of the negotiators that led to collaboration between groups. The element of competition, while continuing somewhat throughout the negotiation session, never really came to the fore—as it normally does in a similar activity—because of the reality of the situation surrounding the petition. The total group seemed earnestly concerned about the best items even though it realized that a petition would not actually be sent to the management. The trainers explained, however, that there would be no restrictions on how individuals chose to act on the issues themselves. Many of the blacks wrote down items on the petition, and some white management visitors made copies of the items when they dropped in during lunch time.

These were the ten items agreed on:

1. Hire more blacks (hire 70 percent blacks until 10 percent of the work force is black).
2. Promote more blacks to supervisory positions.
3. Increase starting wages and adjust unfair rates wherever they occur.
4. Expand sensitivity training to include all levels.

5. Initiate a black-awareness, public-relations program, e.g., a newsletter, a reading library, courses on black culture.

6. Establish a biracial, problem-solving committee, under contract to and elected by employees.

7. Hire more blacks at executive-level positions.

8. Recruit more blacks.

9. Provide *new* programs with blacks in positions of authority so as not to threaten white employees.

10. Evaluate employees annually, send copies to each employee and to his immediate supervisor, and provide job descriptions to serve as guidelines for the evaluations.

A wrap-up session in the afternoon gave whites some understanding of what blacks mean when they say, "That's a cop-out." With blacks observing and whites in the center circle in a fishbowl arrangement, whites were asked, "How do you feel now about your own white racism?" After about fifteen minutes, black participants were asked to take the center of the circle and identify the whites' cop-out statements, which included such things as:

1. I was raised this way and cannot change.

2. Some of my best friends are blacks.

3. I have had blacks working with me and under me for years.

4. I really did not know how bad the situation was.

5. There is not much that any one man can do.

6. I am definitely going to take some action when I get back to the shop.

There seemed to be nothing that whites could do that was not construed as a cop-out. For example, the last statement (#6) was regarded as a cop-out because the speaker did not identify what action he would take, or, if he did, because it would not promote a plant-wide program or policy change.

Finally, whites took the center of the circle again and gave blacks feedback on "This is why I see blacks as hard people to work with." The responses of whites to this task were quite mild. They mentioned that blacks did not listen, that they assumed all whites were enemies, and that they never gave anyone the benefit of the doubt.

The session wound up in a free exchange, in which several blacks regrettably began as they had started on Monday morning with a bitter harangue against whites.

No post-meeting reaction sheets were used to provide an evaluation of the workshop. It did not seem necessary. At the end of the session most people were leery of anything that smacked of academia, of more talk with no action, or of anything that might dissipate the emotional level they had reached.

OUTCOMES

Even a brief experience of this kind of training is an eye-opener for all those who participate. Biracial sessions, in which people take full advantage of a chance to talk openly and frankly with "the other side," expose long-held attitudes to a new appraisal. It is doubtful that anyone can leave these training sessions without having felt considerable impact. In some cases, a degree of understanding of the black situation is achieved on the part of white supervisors, so that they probably do behave in a more constructive, collaborative, and encouraging way with their black subordinates. It is also probably true that initial biases of some participants are only further entrenched.

An unexpected development in these training sessions was the difficulty of doing training exercises with groups composed of black trainees. Research on the life and attitudes of persons in poverty has shown that their thoughts and behavior are directed toward obtaining immediate satisfaction, reducing the amount of talk, and increasing the amount of action. They distrust the workings of bureaucracy and want to go right to the top for immediate decisions. In recent years there has been an increasing pride in minority status, whether it be black, Chicano, Puerto Rican, or simply the status of poverty. Consequently, minorities view with suspicion any efforts that might result in a change of attitudes. They highly resent any behavior or words that might be interpreted as patronizing. Middle-class participants, black *or* white, tend to accept with much greater docility a training activity that requires them to react, to exhibit behaviors, and to think and respond to one another in ways different from everyday life. They can allow themselves to do this for a short period in order to learn from the behavior that has been produced. The hard core often view these training activities as playing games, in the worst sense of the word, or as further efforts to delay action.

The passiveness of the white participants could become a special area of study, leading to implications for problems within society as a whole. The black brothers and the trainees alike took advantage of the training session to harangue whites at great length about their three hundred years of subjugation. Generally, the whites sat there and took it. Whether their lack of response was due to guilt or to a peculiar sense of politeness cannot be determined at this time. Some of their passiveness may have been the result of negative reinforcement. On a few occasions when a white made a protest, he became an immediate target for the blacks, to such an extent that other whites understandably would not want to receive similar treatment. Toward the end of each training period some whites were able to speak more freely, but it was generally noted by that time that they had learned the kind of comments that would be better received by the black participants.

While no real evaluation could be made, it seemed that the learning was a one-way street. That is, the whites undoubtedly learned a great deal about black feelings and attitudes and about their own prejudices, whereas the blacks appeared to learn much less along these lines. No detectable attitude changes were apparent among black participants; the training merely provided them with an outlet for pent-up emotions. The black leadership seemed to appreciate learning about the training techniques, many of which were observed closely so that they could be applied in training programs among other blacks.

Both trainers and management need to consider carefully whether management is willing to make changes as a result of information obtained from such training sessions. Many racist practices that previously may have gone unnoticed are uncovered during training periods. Unless there is an opportunity for this information to be referred to decision makers in management, the result can only be increased frustration among minority members in the work force. It is dysfunctional to set up a situation in which communication is self-contained—people listening only to themselves. A procedure in which management would truly listen and in which the trainees were aware of this would be very helpful. A communication link from a training conference to an ombudsman was one suggestion.

Policy makers in an organization and trainers of lab sessions need to be very clear on their goals for training. Is the training only a means to examine white racism? Is the training only to provide a soundingboard for blacks? Is it only for limited political or economic ends, such as to improve the liberal image of the company? All these ends are dysfunctional in the long run. However, when top management provides overt and continuing support for training programs and makes it clear that changes will be implemented according to the new information obtained, such training sessions can be justified. Policy changes are insufficient; monitoring of practices is necessary.

The employment of minority workers by any large employer carries implications far beyond a minor change in the nature of the work force. It is a wedge that strikes to the heart of individual and corporate attitudes, from the top levels of management to the newest recruits. Complacency is soon shaken, as long-established and well-entrenched policies and practices come under examination and criticism. It cannot be expected that a training program alone will smooth the path for the recruits. Just as changes occur in individuals and communities who forthrightly look at their ways of implementing democracy, so must organizations be prepared to undergo re-evaluation and change as a consequence of learning more about themselves through training programs.

Affirmative Action

DONALD S. GOLDMAN
EUGENE A. CINCOTTA

BACKGROUND

Government and corporate affirmative-action programs have resulted from the growing concern in this country to provide minority groups with jobs and training, thus enabling them to share in the nation's prosperity. Despite recent efforts to implement these programs, however, minority groups often have not felt their impact. This realization prompted one corporation to plan a black-white awareness and confrontation session in order to stimulate understanding of the situation.

Results from affirmative action were almost nil due to the juggling of statistics and lack of cooperation from supervisory personnel. While top management gave at least superficial encouragement to affirmative action, the first-line supervisors—section heads, assistant section heads, and foremen—failed to implement such action.

Six weeks went into the planning of the pilot awareness session. This included selecting the group, obtaining line managerial commitment, financing the program, obtaining the resources, and designing the event. The group decided upon was a "family" group with as many minority participants as possible. This insured attendance and control of the number of participants. Commitment of all involved levels of management was easily obtained once the program plan was presented as being necessary under affirmative action. Financing was made available. Support from an inside, organized black group was obtained, and some personnel were chosen to be used as resources.

Two trainers from industrial relations were in charge of the program. They held an initial meeting with a black pressure group for assistance in planning the awareness session.

Participants

The group selected was the largest engineering laboratory in the division, which had a reputation among black employees as being virtually "lily white." It was decided that the laboratory manager, the business manager, the department manager, and all section heads would participate. In addition to these twelve people, a resource group of six black employees was chosen.

GOALS

It was important for the event to have validity for the participants, to be well planned, to have attainable goals, to be specific, and to be related to needs on the job. The basic experience desired was a chance for supervisors and blacks to exchange dialog with each other. There was also a need to achieve a greater grasp of the issues involved in affirmative action and to set feasible training objectives for carrying out such action.

Assumptions that were being made about race-related attitudes and opinions were questioned early in the planning stages. A meeting of members of the participant group provided a valuable source of information with which to validate assumptions and speculations about the group.

DESIGN

The event took place during one working day and the same evening. Attendance was mandatory.

The morning began with a warm-up activity in which each participant introduced himself and gave a brief description of himself and his expectations for the day. The trainers outlined the purposes of the session.

Three six-person groups were formed—four whites and two blacks in each—to develop lists of questions and concerns and to restate objectives in more relevant ways. This feedback activity facilitated further openness and increased participant ownership. Representatives from each group were chosen to report on issues raised in their group, and notes were recorded on newsprint. Further discussion clarified these issues and indicated direction for the balance of the day. A movie entitled "Black Anger" was shown, followed by participants' reactions and opinions. The balance of the morning was spent exploring race-related feelings and attitudes and learning about the black man's world of work. Fishbowl techniques were employed, using an empty chair, followed by total group discussion.

Participants ate lunch together in a private dining room. Informal discussions were resumed that enabled supervisors to acquire new insights into a variety of social problems facing blacks in corporations. Discussions continued after lunch and black members were asked to relate some of their personal experiences involving racial prejudice—many involving the sponsoring corporation.

Another film, "The Bill of Rights," was shown, followed by discussion and reactions.

A problem from a case study was outlined and the group broke up into role-playing triads, with two white supervisors and one black observer in each. Supervisors selected the role of either department manager or section head and acted out the problem solution, while black employees observed. White supervisors in the role of section heads discussed the problem solution within the triads. Then white supervisors in the role of department managers followed the same procedure. Black observers discussed the process and content of the role play in a fishbowl technique, followed by general discussion by the whole group.

After dinner, lists generated in the morning were checked to determine what progress had been made during the day. Information acquired in previous meetings with supervisors was reported to all participants, followed by a general discussion.

The session concluded with an evaluation and personal comments, including expressions of resentment and appreciation, about the significance of the lab. Finally, participants rated themselves on involvement, using a nine-point scale.

OUTCOMES

As a result of the session, plans for follow-up meetings were approved for the future. Recommendations were also made for additional sessions with other participants.

A one-hour follow-up meeting was held for participants to check whether the level of interest and excitement had waned. It was discovered that feelings were as intense as they had been during the session, if not more so, despite a forecast of lessening demand for manpower.

Hang-Up in Black and White:
A Training Laboratory for
Conflict Identification and Resolution

ARTHUR M. FREEDMAN

BACKGROUND

Concerned over the alleged mistreatment of black Americans by police and National Guard during the aftermath of civil disturbances, the leaders of a Protestant church group in Texas sponsored the creation of the Interreligious Council on Urban Affairs (ICUA), a group composed of concerned clergymen and leaders of several religious faiths. The purpose of the group was to make use of whatever power and influence it had in the city's white communities, in order to prevent similar unnecessary, overzealous retaliation by white officials in the event of further civil disturbances by blacks.

As a first step, the ICUA sought to establish open and meaningful channels of communication with representative black influence groups. It was hoped that improved communications would lead to greater understanding between the black and white communities of the city, which would enable the group to implement some tangible plans. The ICUA invited various black leaders to a series of weekly meetings in order to discuss interracial problems and to make plans for resolving them. However, it soon became evident that the meetings were not fully satisfactory for either the ICUA or the black leaders. The meetings bogged down and their purposes were not achieved.

The ICUA then decided to request consultative help from a consortium of human resource consultants (CHRC). The CHRC agreed to conduct a two-day human relations training laboratory for the ICUA and a representative group of black leaders. The laboratory was intended to identify conflicts and suggest resolutions. It was agreed that the ICUA would assume responsibility for inviting and informing the prospective participants of the purposes and methods of the experience.

Staff

The planning of the lab was conducted under the direction of Philip G. Hanson, Director of the Patients' Training Laboratory at the Houston VA Hospital. The lab staff consisted of Arthur M. Freedman, Jerome B. Brown, and Quentin Dinardo, who all worked with Hanson. All four were members of the CHRC.

Participants

The participants consisted of five blacks and eleven whites. Of the five blacks, four belonged to a privately funded, indigenous community-action program and the fifth worked for a government-sponsored community program.

The black participants were *not* representative of the various black communities in that area. They primarily represented only one of many active influence groups struggling for the uncommitted support of the black (and white) communities.

All eleven whites were members of the ICUA and represented a number of religious denominations; most were clergymen. All participants were men.

GOALS

The overall goals of the lab were to increase awareness and understanding of the attitudes, beliefs, and feelings of the other racial group, and to develop means of maintaining meaningful and durable channels of communication between black and white participants. Specific lab objectives were to facilitate trust between blacks and whites, to examine one's own feelings and attitudes as an individual, to develop more realistic expectations of each other, and to develop positive feelings between black and white participants.

The black participants were primarily concerned with questions of the authenticity of communications between blacks and whites as well as black self-determination. They were vitally interested in whatever help the whites could provide in terms of human and physical resources but, at the same time, they were also concerned with insuring that it would be blacks who decided which direction any collaborative efforts between blacks and whites would or should take, and when such effort should be expended.

DESIGN

The lab was held from dinner on Thursday through dinner on Saturday.

Most of the time was used to focus on the problems (and "hang-ups") that prevented these blacks and whites from working together in a productive manner. Some time was used by the staff to present theoretical material and exercises in order to help participants become more aware of the processes and procedures that either facilitate or interfere with any group's work.

The major portion of the program took place in an unstructured, small-group setting. In this context, many of the attitudes, assumptions, thoughts, and feelings of the participants were identified, explored, and tested in such a way that opportunities were created for the participants to clarify their understandings (1) of themselves as individuals, (2) of the workings of the group with which they were identified, and (3) of what was happening in the other racial group with which they were trying to work. In this manner, it was possible for the groups to create viable and meaningful channels of communication, not only between groups but also within groups. A major part of the process consisted of experimenting with interpersonal behaviors to determine how much trust existed among the participants and whether durable relations could be established between blacks and whites.

As a result of this identification and exploration of the participants' existing attitudes, beliefs, and feelings, the following (paraphrased) statements were expressed:

> I find it very difficult to give you blacks any authentic feedback about what I think and feel about you and the way that you behave, because I'm afraid that if I say anything negative, you'll think that I'm saying it because you're black and I'm prejudiced, and not because you are a *person* who did something that made me angry [about which I chose to become angry]. I'm also afraid that if I give you any positive feedback, you'll think that I'm a patronizing hypocrite who's just trying to manipulate you.

> You white, so-called "liberals" have given me the impression [you behave in such a way that I surmise] that you talk out of both sides of your mouth at the same time. We blacks don't feel that we can *trust* you to mean what you say. We've come to think that you're so concerned about our feelings or your own images that you can't level with us and tell us what your *real* feelings are. That's why we can at least respect people like George Wallace—we hate his guts but at least we *know* where he stands and what his feelings are about us.

> You whites have been making decisions and rules for blacks for the past three hundred years or more—but now, if you want to work with us *at all,* you're going to have to play according to *our* rules. We've *reversed* the rules; now the rule is that you whites do not do anything with us unless *we blacks* are pulling the strings.

Once these ideas and feelings were expressed, it was possible for the participants to explore the implications of their statements and then to establish a more realistic and mutually satisfactory foundation for future collaboration.

OUTCOMES

Seven personal-reaction questions were presented verbally at the last session. The responses to these questions were recorded individually on blank paper. All sixteen participants turned in an answer sheet.[1] The results are summarized briefly below.

1. There was an increase in mutual trust between black and white groups.
2. There was an increase in willingness to be influenced by the other racial group.
3. There was an increased willingness to initiate personal contact with members of the other racial group.
4. There was an increase in empathy and insight into the feelings of the other racial group.
5. There was a greater awareness of the need to utilize the human resources of the other racial group, and an increased willingness to do so.

All increases reported were greater, in all cases, for whites than for blacks. All lab participants felt that the program had helped them understand some of the reasons behind the difficulties that blacks and whites have in communicating with each other in a productive and meaningful manner.

The lab staff believed that greater understanding, more viable channels of communication, more realistic mutual expectations, and some genuine positive feelings were nurtured and developed between black and white participants.

Follow-Up Meetings

Philip Hanson and members of the lab staff attended several formal and informal follow-up meetings between the ICUA and the black group during the six weeks following the lab. These post-lab meetings

---

[1] A complete presentation of all the data can be obtained by request from Philip G. Hanson, VA Hospital, 2002 Holcombe Blvd., Houston, Texas 77031.

were characterized by an atmosphere of considerable openness and trust; individuals were able to confront one another candidly, in a productive manner, when such confrontations arose.

Several of the participants, black and white, expressed feelings that more labs would be helpful. The blacks particularly felt that all-white and all-blacks labs would be a productive prelude to future mixed labs. Such observations and discussions strongly suggest that a large number of the participants felt that the program was useful for them.

From Crisis to Collaboration:
Thoughts on the Use of the Laboratory Method in Resolving Black-White Issues

THOMAS E. WOODALL

BACKGROUND

Because of the increasing polarization of the black and white communities in a major Southern city, a two-day interracial community training project was planned. Black residents of the city, concentrated primarily in a ghetto area, seethed with grievances on a number of issues that placed them in conflict with the city's establishment. A deteriorating situation was created by a high rate of joblessness, inadequate housing, pending displacement of many residents by imminent interstate highway relocation and urban renewal projects (which had been planned without community participation), and charges of favoritism toward powerful business and industrial interests in the renewal projects.

There was little recognition of the differing perceptions and attitudes of either black or white communities on local issues. Communication was highly impersonal and strained. Often both the leaders of the black and white communities would send or carry written messages to the local papers rather than come together to talk directly.

Underlying these concrete problems were deeper factors, perhaps more detrimental to any resolution of the impasse in black-white relations: a lack of trust between blacks and whites, a skepticism on the part of the establishment toward those in the ghetto area, and a clear need for new linkages and extralegal communication channels for more rapid action in times of tension.

Adapted and reprinted from *Social Change: Theory & Application,* Vol. 1, No. 1, 1971, NTL Institute for Applied Behavioral Science, Arlington, Virginia.

Staff

Acting as laboratory coordinator was Orian Worden of Oakland University in Michigan. The training staff also included Richard Franklin of the West Virginia University Appalachian Center.

Participants

The laboratory participants included blacks and whites—the powerful and the powerless—who represented a wide spectrum from government and volunteer sectors. Participants included ghetto high school seniors, the city's mayor, black militants, the urban-renewal director, ministers, community-action workers, a newspaper publisher, the chief of police, and the city planner—in all, about thirty-six.

GOALS

An analysis of the data by staff members indicated the need for a design that would enable participants to learn basic human relations skills; to develop understanding and improve communication and openness across the lines of race, class, and ideology; and to explore solutions to some very real community problems. In response to these goals, the lab was designed to establish an understanding and rapport that could successfully undergird collaboration on back-home concerns.

DESIGN

The lab began on a Saturday morning and ended late Sunday afternoon. It was held in a community center in the heart of the ghetto, a location that created an atmosphere of authenticity and reality. The project used a split design, with one day devoted to opening communication and heightening trust and group decision making, and a second day that stressed work on such crucial community problems as jobs, education, and housing—areas in which miscommunication, frustration, and racial discrimination were most evident.

Saturday morning began with an introduction. Next, during a five-minute period of silent introspection, each participant thought about his own feelings on interracial issues in the city and listed them on paper. This period seemed to be a valuable mechanism for enabling participants to collect their thoughts, to delineate their feelings about racial relationships and community problems, and to prepare themselves for sharing with others. The staff perceived that many of the participants were affected by a high level of initial anxiety. However, by the end of the silent period, participants seemed more receptive to interaction and openness than they had during the initial milling about prior to the lab's opening.

Following the silent introspective stage, participants formed triads to share thoughts and feelings and to get to know one another better. They began to speak quite frankly and openly about very important and personal items in relation to their own racial biases. One white participant told of the racial prejudices of his wife, who for years would not eat in a restaurant in which a Negro was being served, and who scalded the coffee cups after her husband had Negro leaders home for discussions of racial problems. A black told of his son's reluctance to talk about his telephone calls to a white girl because the boy's mother had a negative attitude toward his dating white girls. He also told of the conflict between his two sons, one a moderate, the other a militant who called his brother an Uncle Tom. The chief of police told about his troubles with men on the force who opposed his liberal racial attitudes and policies.

After this, four groups of nine participants each discussed racial attitudes and attempted to establish open communication and understanding. The groups quickly exhibited high rates of participation and involvement. Both the style and the effectiveness of communication between blacks and whites were analyzed. One member of the city administration discovered that it was not what he was saying, but how he was saying it, that was turning off a black community worker; he was coming across as an expert who displayed arrogance toward the opinions and ideas of others. He was helped to see the advantage of modifying his style of communication in order to obtain trust and rapport in his relationships with others.

A white Irish Catholic, whose parents had immigrated to this country, spoke of his experience as a child. He told of a cross being burned on his lawn, and of Ku Klux Klan harassment. As he spoke, tears came to his eyes. These and other confessions seemed to lead to heightened understandings and broadened perspectives on the part of many participants as the day progressed.

During the afternoon a lecturette on feedback and process was given, and the four groups met in clusters to practice observation and feedback with focus on process. The cluster design reinforced awareness of the crucial importance of process in effectively communicating content or informational material to others.

The NASA exercise in group decision making was conducted in the evening. This exercise generated much discussion about the importance of integrating the thinking of a wide spectrum of the community's population into community problem-solving efforts.

By this time many new insights into the human factors underlying interracial and community problems had been generated and shared by the members. The participants had also moved through a sequence of phases, going from a heterogeneous collection of individuals to a relatively cohesive, unified group. In doing so, they had become willing to share their individual differences and similarities, to attempt to build trust, to help one another with their individual problems, and finally to collaborate on a common task in a consensual exercise. It seemed that they were more prepared for Sunday's focus on the real world of back-home problems.

Sunday morning's design called for a problem census by the total group, which resulted in the identification of three specific problem areas as most crucial: housing, employment, and education. On a self-selective basis, groups were formed around these three general areas. The groups were of nearly equal size, and they spent the morning attempting to define and solve particular problems.

On Sunday afternoon, the groups continued to work on their problem areas until just before closing time, when a total community sharing took place. It became apparent by mid-afternoon that the employment group was the most advanced of the three, and the other groups joined it to provide consultation in their efforts to come up with viable solutions. The result was a plan to involve policy makers in business, industry, and labor in alleviating the plight of the jobless and the unemployed in the city. The mayor made a commitment to obtain the support of business and industrial leaders in an all-out effort to create new jobs before the long hot summer began.

OUTCOMES

The final design component was a general sharing by all participants. It became clear that a great deal had resulted from the experience. One militant high school senior said that she had had an opportunity to discover that the mayor was not just a man who sat behind a desk and signed his name. Both blacks and whites expressed deepened perspectives and increased understanding of the other side. New communication linkages and coalitions had been formed. People who previously had felt hostile toward one another were now talking. Those holding power saw that they might share some of the power and not be inundated by radical revolutionaries; the powerless had been able to taste a sense of the potential of collaboration with the power structure.

The summer passed without major disruptions or expressions of hostility between blacks and whites in the city. The mayor and his administration, working with local business and industrial leaders, launched a successful drive to provide summer job opportunities to ghetto youngsters in the city's stores, factories, and government departments.

Building on the relationship established with the high school student in the lab, the mayor and his human-rights commissioner were instrumental in organizing interracial student advisory committees in each city high school. Working with local school officials, they also supported the creation of advisory committees of black and white parents to maintain communications with the commission on potentially troublesome racial issues.

Supported by the mayor and the human-rights commissioner, the chief of police initiated a community-relations training program for his force, utilizing a laboratory training approach and involving community leaders from both the ghetto and the white community.

City officials were able to use new communication linkages and increased trust and understanding with a wider segment of the ghetto population in aborting a potentially explosive confrontation between ghetto residents and interstate relocation officials during the summer.

Apparently, the lab provided an impetus and a mechanism for significant advances in the city's interracial climate.

Structured Experiences: Personal and Interpersonal

Getting Acquainted and Warm-Up

Listing Exercise: Confronting Personal Responses

Goals

    I. To clarify one's personal feelings toward members of a particular minority or other group.

    II. To identify personal styles and preferences in expressing or not expressing these feelings.

    III. To discover any inconsistencies in personal behavior toward members of that group and the implications of such inconsistencies.

    IV. To identify assumptions, behaviors, and conditions that hinder or facilitate authentic interpersonal relations.

Group Size

Unlimited numbers of groups of five or six participants each.

Time Required

Approximately one and one-half hours.

Submitted by David A. Landy.

Materials

    I. Three sheets of paper and a pencil for each participant.

    II. Newsprint and a felt-tipped marker.

Physical Setting

A room large enough for groups to interact without distractions from other groups.

Process

    I. The facilitator explains that the initial task is to gain an awareness of personal responses to members of a particular group in order to provide real data for learning.

    II. He then distributes three sheets of paper and a pencil to each participant and forms groups of five or six participants each. (It is probably more effective to form groups of individuals who do not regularly interact with one another.)

    III. The facilitator asks each participant to generate a list on the topic "What I like *most* about myself in relation to members of this minority group." He may wish to write the topic on newsprint.

    IV. When five minutes has passed, he asks the participants to share their lists with others in their group and to discuss the implications of the lists. (Twenty minutes.)

    V. The facilitator asks each participant to generate a list on the topic "What I like *least* about myself in relation to this group." When five minutes has passed, he asks participants to share with others as before.

    VI. The facilitator leads the participants in a general discussion of the new learnings derived from the list-making and sharing experience. He suggests that the laboratory setting in which they are presently involved encourages growth through experimentation with new behaviors. He asks them to rejoin their groups in order to generate a third personal list of *new* behaviors they wish to try involving interactions between themselves and the members of the specific group.

    VII. When these lists are completed the facilitator asks participants to help each other develop strategies for implementing experiments with new behaviors. He may ask participants to form helping pairs and to make explicit contracts with each other about their intended behavior. (If the laboratory includes interaction with members of the specified group, the strategies should reflect this, and the facilitator should design the laboratory to accommodate the needs of the participants toward experimentation.)

VIII. The facilitator suggests that participants approach this task by asking themselves the following questions:
1. What will make it difficult to engage in these new behaviors?
2. What will facilitate engaging in these new behaviors?

Controversial Statements:
A Getting-Acquainted Rap

Goals

I. To facilitate a rapid sense of belonging within the group.

II. To generate a discussion on racial issues in a nonthreatening way.

III. To give participants a sense of where others stand on racial issues both intellectually and emotionally.

IV. To allow participants an opportunity to monitor their own reactions during a discussion concerning racial issues.

Group Size

Groups of nine to twelve are optimal. Larger groups may impede free interaction during the discussion.

Time Required

A minimum of one hour.

Materials

I. Newsprint and felt-tipped markers.

II. A copy of the Controversial Statements Sheet for each participant.

Physical Setting

A room in which chairs can be placed in a circle to encourage eye contact and group cohesiveness, and newsprint placed where all can readily see the topics.

Process

I. The facilitator asks participants to form pairs by selecting someone they know least well.

II. Members of each pair are instructed to interview each other for the next ten minutes and to be prepared to introduce their partner to the group. The facilitator suggests that they ask each other about any convenient subject, such as leisure-time interests, their families, or their jobs.

III. When the interviews are finished, each participant takes one to three minutes to introduce his partner to the group, telling a little of what he has learned about his partner during the interview.

IV. The facilitator then leads a short discussion on how the participants feel about the interviewing experience.

V. The facilitator explains that they will now engage in a discussion of controversial topics concerning racial issues. He urges them to participate freely in the discussions and to be alert to the responses of themselves and of others in the group to the topics and the opinions of those around them.

VI. The facilitator distributes copies of the Controversial Statements Sheet. Participants select statements from the sheet and solicit reactions to them. Members are encouraged to discuss each selected statement before moving to the next item.

VII. When the experience is concluded, the facilitator asks participants to describe any new learnings they have experienced from the activity in terms of increased knowledge, insights into others, and insights into themselves. These are listed on newsprint, and a final discussion on the implications of these new learnings is conducted.

Controversial Statements Sheet

1. Black Power has done more to hurt blacks than to help them.
2. With all the jobs available, anyone who wants to work can find a job.
3. Violence in the cities is caused primarily by outside agitators.
4. Before we can have social justice, we must first have law and order.
5. If blacks really wanted to move up, they would stay in school.
6. One of the problems today is the apathy of blacks.
7. If we really integrate the schools, we must accept a lowering of educational standards.
8. It is as easy today to work your way up as it was for the immigrant groups.
9. The welfare system needs investigation to correct "coddling" and "fraud."
10. Unwed mothers who continue to have illegitimate children should be placed in jail.
11. The police could control violence if their hands were not tied by recent Supreme Court decisions.
12. Professional workers know best what is beneficial for the poor.
13. Keeping whites out of the civil rights movement will prevent any real progress.
14. One of the major causes of civil disorder is white racism.
15. Blacks have made a lot of progress in recent years.
16. Bussing ghetto children is only going to antagonize the white community and make the situation worse.
17. Blacks ought to get equal treatment, but it is not fair to give them preference over whites for jobs and promotions.
18. Property values always go down when a black buys a home in a white neighborhood.
19. Interracial marriage is a threat to most white Americans.
20. Interracial marriage is all right for the couple, but presents overwhelming problems for the children.
21. Private clubs should have the right to exclude people for racial or religious reasons.

22. The examples of men like Senator Brooke, Ralph Bunche, and Thurgood Marshall prove that blacks have equal opportunity and treatment.

23. The government cannot legislate morality; changes in the racial situation will have to start in the hearts of men.

24. Every white person in this room is justified in feeling superior to any black in the world.

Food for Thought:
A Black-Identity Questionnaire

Goals

    I. To help black participants evaluate their own perceptions of identity.

    II. To help put each participant in touch with his particular reality as a black person.

Group Size

Any number of groups of six or eight participants each.

Time Required

Approximately one and one-half hours.

Materials

    I. A copy of the Food for Thought Questionnaire for each participant.

    II. Pencils.

    III. 5" × 8" cards and pins (optional).

Physical Setting

A room large enough for groups to work separately.

Process

    I. The facilitator distributes pencils and copies of the Food for Thought Questionnaire and instructs participants to complete the questionnaire.

    II. When the questionnaires have been completed, the facilitator forms participants into groups of six or eight.

    III. The facilitator directs participants to read their self-descriptions of four words to their group and to explain why they feel that this particular set of adjectives best describes their

---

Submitted by Jerry Klein and Roy Thompson.

personal identities. As each participant makes his explanation, the other members of the group are free to challenge him in his choice. Any modifications in the self-description must be made by consensual agreement of the group, including the member under discussion. Further modifications can be made during the experience as more data about the participant come to light. As participants gain new insights into themselves in terms of identity, they can suggest modifications that will be processed consensually by the group.

IV. Participants are then instructed to pair off within their subgroups. Members of the pairs discuss their answers to question 1 of the Food for Thought Questionnaire. Participants are to re-evaluate their answers in terms of their current self-descriptions and to help each other see additional advantages and/or question the relevance of listed advantages.

V. When question 1 has been discussed, the facilitator asks participants to pair off with a new partner within the group and to share the information under question 2 in the same manner as before.

VI. This process continues until each participant has met with four partners and has completed discussion of his questionnaire responses.

VII. The facilitator asks each group to repeat the process for step III, emphasizing new insights into each participant's identity. (He may ask participants to wear identity tags for the remainder of the workshop and may encourage further feedback about an individual's behavior in the group compared with his statement of identity. A suggested format for the tags might be: "I am a militant black middle-class student.")

Food for Thought Questionnaire

Part I. Identity

Circle one item in each column that best describes you.

Column 1	Column 2	Column 3	Column 4
Militant	Afro-American	Lower-Class	Business Person
Liberal	Negro	Middle-Class	White-Collar Worker
Conservative	Black	Upper-Class	Professional
Indifferent	African		Blue-Collar Worker
	Other_____		Student
			Laborer
			Other_____

Write the four items you have chosen on the line below.

I best describe myself as a (an)

_____   _____   _____   _____.

Part II. Advantages and Disadvantages

With the previous description in mind, write a brief answer to each of the following questions:

1. What are the advantages of being this kind of person in the black community?

2. What are the advantages of being this kind of person in the white community in which you must function?

3. What are the disadvantages of being this kind of person in the black community?

4. What are the disadvantages of being this kind of person in the white community in which you must function?

Social Barometer:
A Value-Clarification Activity

Goals

I. To help participants clarify their own value positions on a variety of social, cultural, and political issues.

II. To observe the group's diversity and clustering of opinions on a variety of subjects.

Group Size

Unlimited.

Time Required

Approximately one hour, depending on the size of the group and the number of barometer cues utilized.

Materials

I. A copy of the Social Barometer Cues Sheet for each participant.

II. Eleven 8½″ × 11″ sheets of paper, each clearly marked with one of the following barometer indicators: −100, −80, −60, −40, −20, 0, +20, +40, +60, +80, +100. These sheets are positioned (e.g., taped to a wall or the floor) at least two feet apart.

Physical Setting

A room large enough for participants to gather at various points along the social barometer.

Process

I. The facilitator explains that participants will have the opportunity to explore their feelings regarding certain social, cultural, and political terms and issues by physically placing themselves along the indicators of the social barometer. Three participants

---

Adapted by permission from materials prepared by Thomas Azumbrado in *Intergroup Education & Social Change*. Brooklyn: Board of Education of the City of New York, 1970.

at a time will react to an issue until all have had an opportunity to participate.

II. The facilitator asks for three volunteers to illustrate the process. The three people line up in front of the zero indicator of the social barometer to begin the procedure. The facilitator calls out a cue word, "beer," from the Social Barometer Cues Sheet and asks the three people to position themselves at the indicator that best corresponds to their personal like or dislike for that stimulus. For example, if the participant likes beer very much, he should stand in the vicinity of +80 to +100. Neutrality on an issue would be the position zero.

III. The facilitator calls for three participants at a time to react to each cue until all have participated in the activity for that term. Cues can be chosen in any manner desired, and the facilitator may add other relevant cues to the cues sheet.

IV. When all participants are familiar with the process, the facilitator allows participants to call out their own cue words, heightening the emotional environment of the experience. He asks that participants monitor their own responses to the cues and their reactions to the positions of others on the barometer. No one is forced to defend his position on an issue. (Discussions of the issues themselves should be avoided until later in the activity.)

V. The barometer phase of the experience concludes with a discussion of the participants' responses to the issues and their reactions to the positions chosen by themselves and others. The facilitator may wish to draw upon this experience in focusing the workshop beyond this introductory activity, or he may ask participants to develop an agenda for a workshop based on this initial experience.

Social Barometer Cues Sheet

Beer
Baseball
Yourself
Technology
Automation
Guaranteed income
Unions
Boycotts
Demonstrations
Administrators
Supervisors
Subordinates
On-the-job training
  for supervisors
Training the
  untrained worker
The unemployed
Public welfare
Preferential treatment
  for the poor
Anti-poverty programs
Black self-determinism
Black power
White blacklash

Black capitalism
Ghettos
Suburbs
The Mafia
Birth control
Premarital sex
Abortion
Extramarital sex
Prostitution
Jewish president of U.S.
Black president of U.S.
Democrats
Republicans
The President of U.S.
Radical groups
Participatory democracy
Community control
Capitalism
Free enterprise system
Bureaucracy
Federal aid
States rights
The military

Intergroup Awareness and Communication

Intergroup Perceptions:
An Introductory Feedback Experience

Goal

To generate discussion of various ethnic, social, or political groups' perceptions of themselves, of others, and of others' views of them.

Group Size

Unlimited.

Time Required

Approximately one hour.

Materials

Paper, pencils, newsprint, felt-tipped markers, and masking tape for each subgroup.

Physical Setting

A room large enough to accommodate the various subgroups comfortably without one group distracting another, or one room large enough for total group discussion and smaller rooms for subgroup meetings.

Process

    I. The facilitator suggests to the total group that behavior depends to a large extent on one's self-perception and one's perception of others.

II. He asks participants to form groups based on their ethnic, social, or political allegiances (depending on the objectives of the workshop). When the groups have been assembled, the facilitator distributes writing and posting materials to each group and asks it to describe the attributes it believes are characteristic of each of the other groups. He suggests that each group brainstorm a list of characteristics and record them, then discuss the characteristics, compile a final list by consensus, and record it on newsprint.

III. When the groups have completed this first task, the facilitator asks each group to describe what it believes other groups' perceptions of its group will be. This task is accomplished in the same way as the first task.

IV. The facilitator then brings all participants together. A representative from each subgroup posts and reads the characteristics his group compiled of each of the other groups. Participants are not to respond at this time.

V. Next the representatives post and read the descriptions of how their group believes other groups perceive them.

VI. The facilitator then leads a discussion of the discrepancies and misperceptions among the various subgroups. While care is taken to avoid minimizing real differences between groups, common characteristics among groups are also noted and their implications discussed.

Racial Awareness:
A Black-White Communications Experience

Goals

    I. To determine verbal expressions of blacks and whites that produce negative emotional responses and hinder interracial communication.

    II. To give participants in a black-white workshop an opportunity to become resources for one another in understanding verbal communication.

Group Size

Any number of participants, preferably equal numbers of blacks and whites.

Time Required

Approximately one and one-half hours.

Materials

    I. Tape recorder.

    II. Pencils and paper.

    III. A copy of the Racial Awareness Statements Sheet for each participant.

    IV. Newsprint and a felt-tipped marker.

Physical Setting

A large room in which several small groups can meet without excessive distractions.

Process

    I. Prior to the session, the facilitator records on tape the statements from the Racial Awareness Statements Sheet, using

---

Submitted by Gail Silverman.

a variety of voices, e.g., black, white; male, female; Southern, Northern. He may ask workshop participants to assist him in the taping. (Statements other than those included on the sheet may be substituted if they seem more relevant to the design of the workshop or the particular client group.)

II. The facilitator explains to participants that they will be asked to share their emotional responses to racial statements. He suggests that more effective interracial communication occurs when individuals become aware of their own "hang-ups" and limitations. (This is not an appropriate time for participants to suspend personal racial feelings in order to appear agreeable, tolerant, or liberal; the purpose is to develop insight into one's own reactions.)

III. Pencils and paper are distributed. The facilitator asks black participants to line up across the room and white participants to line up facing them at a distance of two feet. He tells them that he will play a recording of various statements dealing with race and that they are to take one step backward if the statement creates any amount of tension, anger, or defensiveness in them. Participants should monitor their emotional responses carefully and be honest during the experience. After each statement, participants make notes about their feelings.

IV. After the twenty-four statements have been read, participants are asked to observe the physical distance that now exists between the two racial groups.

V. All participants form one large group to discuss briefly how this dramatization illustrates problems in communication between blacks and whites.

VI. The facilitator forms small groups (six or eight members each) of approximately equal numbers of blacks and whites.

VII. The facilitator distributes the Racial Awareness Statements Sheets to participants.

VIII. He assigns each group an equal number of black and white statements and asks the members of each group to become resources for one another in exploring these statements in terms of three emphases: (1) historical focus (what created this attitude); (2) language patterns (what "soul," for example, really means); and (3) personal experiences ("Everyone was my 'friend' in the dorm, but I was never asked to a party"). The facilitator posts these three emphases on news-print.

IX. Each participant is asked to write down new insights into his racial awareness that emerge during this process. The facilitator asks each group to discuss means of attaining better interracial communication.

X. Participants reassemble for a general discussion of approaches to better understanding and communication. The facilitator inquires how these approaches might best be implemented. During this discussion, he emphasizes openness and willing-ness to offer and to receive feedback. Generalizations from this discussion are posted.

Racial Awareness Statements Sheet

Black Statements

1. You'd better not drive your hog out there; yours looks better than his.
2. You can't fight city hall; they just don't give a damn.
3. They should get off our backs.
4. Well, they've sent another one out here to solve our problems, and they don't even know our problems!
5. For a man with a degree, he's damn ignorant about black folks.
6. I don't want to be one of them; I just want to be able to go any place I can afford to go.
7. I'm not colored; I was born this way.
8. I'm tired of honkies experimenting on me.
9. I'm no Negro, I'm a soul brother.
10. I don't want to socialize with them, I just want to be able to go where I want, when I want.
11. They just try to razzle-dazzle you with words.
12. If there is one thing I can't stand, it's an Uncle Tom, and on top of that, one of those Oreos.

White Statements

1. They sure have rhythm.
2. They can't even agree among themselves about what they want.
3. As soon as one moves in, the neighborhood goes down.
4. Why change anything? They're happy the way they are.
5. I asked our maid, and she doesn't agree with all those black power people.
6. Some of my best friends are blacks.
7. They all look alike to me.
8. Would you want your daughter to marry one?
9. It's not that I'm prejudiced; I just like to be with people of my own kind.
10. They should ship them all back to Africa.
11. There are some living on the next block from us, but they know their place.
12. You've got to be black to get a job these days.

Whiteness:
Racial Perceptions Through Color Associations

Goal

To increase white participants' awareness of color perceptions as they affect racial attitudes.

Group Size

Any number of participants that can be divided into subgroups of eight to twelve participants.

Time Required

Approximately one and one-half hours.

Materials

    I. Newsprint and a felt-tipped marker.

    II. A copy of the Whiteness Questions Sheet for each participant.

    III. A copy of the Whiteness Rating Sheet for each participant.

    IV. Pencils.

Physical Setting

A room large enough to accommodate small groups comfortably without excessive noise distractions.

Process

    I. The facilitator explains that he will ask three questions concerning a certain color. Participants are to respond quickly by calling out the first adjective or association that comes to mind. As the responses are made, the facilitator lists them on newsprint. The three questions are: "What comes to mind when you think of the color *red*? What comes to mind when you think of a *red* person? What do you think of when you think of a *red* group?"

    II. The same process is repeated with the following colors: yellow, green, blue, and black.

III. The facilitator leads a brief discussion concerning the insights gained through the experience, emphasizing the tendency toward stereotyped responses.

IV. The facilitator forms subgroups of approximately eight participants and distributes pencils and copies of the Whiteness Questions Sheet to each group. Participants respond independently to the five questions on the sheet.

V. Each group chooses a moderator to pose the questions and to record themes in the group members' responses to them. (Twenty minutes.)

VI. When each group has finished discussing the questions, the facilitator directs each group to write a consensus statement beginning with, "Being white means . . ." (Five minutes.)

VII. The facilitator distributes a copy of the Whiteness Rating Sheet to each participant. He instructs participants to complete the ratings using the consensus statement as the criteria for the rating.

VIII. Each participant solicits feedback of the ratings from the other members of his group. Then he gives his own self-ratings and discusses his reactions.

IX. The subgroups reassemble for a general sharing of reactions to the experience. Consensus statements are published and personal learnings are shared.

Whiteness Questions Sheet

1. What is white?

2. What does it mean to be white?

3. How white am I?

4. How do I experience my whiteness?

5. When do I feel most white?

Consensus Statement: Being white means . . .

Whiteness Rating Sheet

My Ratings of Myself and Other Group Members:

1. I perceive my whiteness to be:

   Least white   1   2   3   4   5   6   7   8   9   10   Most white

2. Others in my group probably perceive my whiteness to be:

   Least white   1   2   3   4   5   6   7   8   9   10   Most white

3. I perceive the whiteness of others in my group to be:

   Least white   1   2   3   4   5   6   7   8   9   10   Most white

My Ratings for Individual Group Members:

1. I perceive the whiteness of _____ to be:

   Least white   1   2   3   4   5   6   7   8   9   10   Most white

2. I perceive the whiteness of _____ to be:

   Least white   1   2   3   4   5   6   7   8   9   10   Most white

3. I perceive the whiteness of _____ to be:

   Least white   1   2   3   4   5   6   7   8   9   10   Most white

4. I perceive the whiteness of _____ to be:

   Least white   1   2   3   4   5   6   7   8   9   10   Most white

5. I perceive the whiteness of _____ to be:

   Least white   1   2   3   4   5   6   7   8   9   10   Most white

6. I perceive the whiteness of _____ to be:

   Least white   1   2   3   4   5   6   7   8   9   10   Most white

7. I perceive the whiteness of _____ to be:

   Least white   1   2   3   4   5   6   7   8   9   10   Most white

8. I perceive the whiteness of _____ to be:

   Least white   1   2   3   4   5   6   7   8   9   10   Most white

My Ratings by Group Members:

On the scale below record the *name* of each other group member at the point on the scale corresponding to the rating that each assigns to you.

Other group members perceive my whiteness to be:

Least white   1 2 3 4 5 6 7 8 9 10   Most white

Blocking and Facilitating:
An Awareness-Expansion Activity

Goals

    I. To increase one's awareness of assumptions about authentic black-white interpersonal relations.

    II. To increase awareness of behaviors that either block or facilitate authentic interpersonal relationships between blacks and whites.

Group Size

Any number of participants, preferably equal numbers of blacks and whites.

Time Required

Two hours.

Materials

    I. A copy of the Blocking and Facilitating Assumptions and Behaviors Sheet for each participant.

    II. Paper and pencils for each participant.

    III. Newsprint and a felt-tipped marker.

Physical Setting

A room large enough to accommodate participants comfortably.

Process

    I. The facilitator distributes the Blocking and Facilitating Assumptions and Behaviors Sheets to participants and asks them to consider the first category, Assumptions That Block Authentic Relations.

Adapted and reprinted from Bertram M. Lee and Warren H. Schmidt, "Toward More Authentic Interpersonal Relations Between Blacks and Whites," *Human Relations Training News,* Vol. 13, No. 4, NTL Institute for Applied Behavioral Science, Washington, D.C., pp. 4–5. Permission granted by the publisher and the authors.

II. Then the facilitator asks the participants to offer additional assumptions based on their own experience. As suggestions are made, the facilitator writes them on newsprint.

III. Each of the other three categories (Assumptions That Facilitate Authentic Relations, Behaviors That Block Authentic Relations, and Behaviors That Facilitate Authentic Relations) is considered in the same fashion.

IV. Next, the facilitator asks two black and two white participants to form a discussion group. He arranges the other participants in a circle around the discussion group as observers. He may also elect to use an "open chair" to encourage more participation.

V. The facilitator allows fifteen minutes for the group to discuss the importance of the assumptions included in the first category—as well as those added by participants—with regard to their particular roles as administrators, parents, businessmen, individuals, or whatever best relates to them as a group. After the discussion, brief comments are elicited from the observers.

VI. The facilitator selects a new group of two black and two white participants to discuss the assumptions in the second category. This pattern continues until all four categories have been discussed.

VII. The facilitator distributes pencils and paper to the participants. He asks each person to devise an individual agenda based on assumption and behavior changes that will facilitate his interracial interactions with others.

VIII. Participants form interracial pairs to discuss these personal agendas. The facilitator instructs the members of each pair to assist each other by suggesting methods of changing behavior or assumptions.

Blocking and Facilitating Assumptions and Behaviors Sheet

I. Assumptions That Block Authentic Relations

Assumptions Whites Make:

1. Color is unimportant in interpersonal relations.
2. Blacks will always welcome and appreciate inclusion in white society.
3. Open recognition of color may embarrass blacks.
4. Blacks are trying to use whites.
5. Blacks can be stereotyped.
6. White society is superior to black society.
7. Liberal whites are free of racism.
8. All blacks are alike in their attitudes and behavior.
9. Blacks are oversensitive.
10. Blacks must be controlled.

Assumptions Blacks Make:

1. All whites are alike.
2. There are no "soul brothers" among whites.
3. Honkies have all the power.
4. Whites are always trying to use blacks.
5. Whites are united in their attitude toward blacks.
6. All whites are racists.
7. Whites are not really trying to understand the situation of blacks.
8. Whitey has got to deal on black terms.
9. Silence is a sign of hostility.
10. Whites cannot and will not change, except by force.
11. The only way to gain attention is through confrontation.
12. All whites are deceptive.
13. All whites will let you down in the "crunch."

II. Assumptions That Facilitate Authentic Relations

Assumptions Whites Make:

1. People count as individuals.
2. Blacks are human—with individual feelings, aspirations, and attitudes.
3. Blacks have a heritage of which they are proud.
4. Interdependence is needed between blacks and whites.
5. Blacks are angry.
6. Whites cannot fully understand what it means to be black.
7. Whiteness/blackness is a real difference, but not the basis on which to determine behavior.
8. Most blacks can handle whites' authentic behavior and feelings.
9. Blacks want a responsible society.
10. Blacks are capable of managerial maturity.
11. I may be part of the problem.

Assumptions Blacks Make:

1. Openness is healthy.
2. Interdependence is needed between blacks and whites.
3. People count as individuals.
4. Negotiation and collaboration are possible strategies.
5. Whites are human beings and, whether they should or not, have their own hang-ups.
6. Some whites can help by doing their own thing.
7. Some whites have "soul."

III. Behaviors That Block Authentic Relations

Behaviors of Whites:

1. Interrupting blacks when they talk.
2. Condescending behavior.
3. Offering help where not needed or wanted.
4. Avoidance of contact (eye-to-eye and physical).
5. Verbal focus on black behavior rather than on white behavior.
6. Insisting on playing games according to white rules.
7. Showing annoyance at blacks' behavior that differs from their own.
8. Too-easy expressions of acceptance and friendship.
9. Talking about—rather than to—blacks who are present.

Behaviors of Blacks:

1. Confrontation too early and too harshly.
2. Rejection of honest expressions of acceptance and friendship.
3. Pushing whites into such a defensive posture that learning and re-examination are impossible.
4. Failure to keep a commitment and then offering no explanation.
5. In-group joking, laughing at whites—in black-culture language.
6. Giving answers blacks think whites want to hear.
7. Using confrontation as the primary relationship style.
8. Isolationism.

IV. Behaviors That Facilitate Authentic Relations

Behaviors of Whites:

1. Directness and openness in expressing feelings.
2. Assisting other whites to understand and to confront feelings.
3. Supporting self-initiated moves of black people.
4. Listening without interrupting.
5. Demonstrating interest in learning about black perceptions, culture, etc.
6. Staying with and working through difficult confrontations.
7. Taking risks, e.g., being first to confront the differences.
8. Assuming responsibility for examining their own motives.

Behaviors of Blacks:

1. Showing interest in understanding whites' point of view.
2. Acknowledging that there are some whites committed to bettering interracial relations.
3. Acting as if blacks have some power—and do not need to prove it.
4. Allowing whites to experience unaware areas of racism.
5. Openness.
6. Expression of real feelings.
7. Dealing with whites on their terms.
8. Meeting whites half way.
9. Treating whites on a one-to-one basis.
10. Telling it like it is.
11. Realistic goal sharing.
12. Showing pride in their heritage.

Fantasies

Identity Fantasies: Clarifying Stereotypes

Goals

I. To help each person focus on his identity as it relates to stereo-typed views of groups in society.

II. To help each person understand his emotional responses to being stereotyped.

Group Size

Any number of groups of about eight participants each. (One staff member is needed per group.)

Time Required

Approximately two hours.

Physical Setting

A room large enough to seat everyone comfortably; ideally, a carpeted room where participants can lie down during the fantasies.

Process

I. The facilitator may use one or two brief fantasies as a warm-up. He asks the participants to close their eyes and tells them

Submitted by Peter S. Caffentzis.

to imagine that they are entering a room where a voice will speak to them. They are to respond silently to the voice with the first thought that occurs to them. The facilitator says, "The voice asks 'Who are you?'" He pauses and continues: "The voice now asks 'Why?' Answer it. [Pause.] It is asking 'Why?' again. Each time you answer, it repeats 'Why?' Continue this dialog with the voice, answering the question 'Why?' in as many ways as you can." Five minutes is allowed for the fantasy to continue.

II. The facilitator allows sufficient time for as many people as possible to report on their experiences. No evaluations are to be made by anyone.

III. The facilitator then asks the participants to close their eyes while they fantasize the following experience: "We are going to take a walk. At a certain point in the walk, I am going to stop and ask you to make a choice. We are all walking and laughing together in a sunlit meadow. Take your shoes off. Doesn't the cool grass feel good under your feet? The sun is warm, but there is just a little breeze to refresh us. Let's walk over to the left where those yellow and blue wildflowers are growing. Pick one. [Pause.] Can you smell that delicate scent? Share your flower with another member of the group. [Pause.] We are approaching a hill now. We startle some pheasants. Look at their vivid colors as they fly off to the right. We are climbing the hill and, as we reach the crest, we see five gates below us. Over each gate is a sign. One gate is labeled Protestant, one Catholic, one Jewish, one Black, and one White." (The facilitator should choose gate labels that are most relevant to the participant group.) "Now you are on your own. Select the gate through which you wish to pass and imagine what you will find on the other side." The facilitator allows three minutes for the participants to complete the fantasy.

IV. The facilitator again gives everyone sufficient time to report on his experiences, and again no evaluations are made.

V. When the discussion is finished, the facilitator asks the participants to close their eyes and to imagine that they have re-formed as a group. "We are walking again down a sunlit slope toward a building. We enter the building and begin walking down a corridor. Look over to your left through the large window. All the people you see through this window are Catholic. What do they look like? What are they doing?" (The facilitator allows approximately one minute for this phase of the fantasy.) "Let's move down the hall. Stop at the large window on your right. All the people you see through this window are black. What do they look like? What are they doing?" The facilitator continues the fantasy until each group has been seen through the windows. He ends the fantasy by taking the group out of the building and into the meadow again.

VI. As before, the facilitator asks people to report on their experiences, but he ends the discussion after three minutes. He then forms groups of about eight persons each. One staff member is assigned to each group.

VII. Each staff member begins by asking the participants if they actually got back to the sunlit meadow after the experience of being in the building. (Many participants never leave the building.) The staff member encourages discussion of the entire experience as fully as possible, helping the participants integrate any new insights into their personal identities. It may be helpful for those who did not experience coming back into the sunlit meadow to talk about the point at which they departed from the group fantasy. The function of the staff member is to encourage each participant to focus on any conflict between who he is and who he would like to be. (People need to understand that conflict is a natural element in human growth.)

Rebirth Fantasy:
Discovering Racist Attitudes and Stereotypes

Goal

To help each person become aware of his own racist attitudes.

Group Size

Any number of groups of four to six people each, preferably equal numbers of blacks and whites.

Time Required

Approximately two and one-half hours.

Materials

    I. A copy of the Rebirth Fantasy Guide for each participant.

    II. Newsprint and felt-tipped markers.

Physical Setting

A room large enough to accommodate several subgroups comfortably, with minimal distractions, or one room large enough for all participants to meet together and smaller rooms for subgroup meetings.

Process

    I. The facilitator explains that participants will consider the accuracy of their views about different minority or ethnic groups.

    II. He asks them to close their eyes while he leads them through a fantasy designed to help focus on their views. He explains that each white participant is to imagine that he has been reborn as a black infant. Each black participant is to imagine that he has been reborn as a white infant. (The fantasy can be modified to pertain to the appropriate minority groups represented.)

Submitted by Arthur M. Freedman and Jerry Perlmutter.

III. The facilitator slowly reads the Rebirth Fantasy Guide, allowing the participants to develop their fantasies in as vivid and elaborate a manner as possible without taking an excessive amount of time.

IV. When the fantasy has been concluded, he asks the participants to form groups of four to six members of their own race. He distributes copies of the Rebirth Fantasy Guide, newsprint, and felt-tipped markers to each group.

V. The facilitator asks each group to develop and record on newsprint a composite list of its responses to each of the Rebirth Fantasy Guide questions and to disregard any inconsistencies. One hour is allowed for completion of the composite lists.

VI. Each group then exchanges its composite for that of a different racial group and evaluates it. Then each group develops a list of racist attitudes and stereotypes that it believes are contained either implicitly or explicitly in the other group's composite.

VII. The facilitator asks the participants to form two large groups, one black and one white. He asks each group to formulate a final list of approximately ten of the most prevalent racist attitudes or stereotypes it has discovered.

VIII. When the final lists are completed, they are posted. Participants form a single group again to discuss the lists in terms of the goals of the workshop. The facilitator may focus the discussion by asking participants to complete the following statements (in sequence):
1. "I have learned . . ." (theory building)
2. "As I *now* reflect on how I have acted toward people from other races, I remind myself . . ." (application)
3. "When I return to my own back-home situation, I will . . ." (commitment to action).

Rebirth Fantasy Guide

You Are an Infant:

1. What are your physical surroundings like?

2. What is your life like in your family?

3. Can you see your mother? father? sisters? brothers? other relatives?

4. What kind of people are they?

5. Who takes care of you?

You Are a Child:

1. What kind of clothes are you wearing?

2. Who are your friends?

3. How does your black (white) body feel to you?

4. What do you do with your friends?

5. What is your life with your family like now?

You Are an Adolescent:

1. Who are the most important people in your neighborhood?

2. What do you want to do when you get older?

3. What is your neighborhood community like? Do you like the way it looks? smells?

4. How would you like to live?

5. What kind of world is this?

6. How long do you go to school? Why do you leave? How old are you when you leave?

7. Have you ever met a black (white) person?

8. What do you think about black (white) people?

You Are an Adult:

1. What kind of work do you do to make money?
2. How many jobs have you had?
3. Do you feel that you have any value to other people?
4. Are you married?
5. Do you have any children?
6. What is your married life like?
7. What kind of life do you think your children will have?
8. What will their futures be like?
9. Are you getting everything you want in your life?
10. What do you do in your neighborhood?
11. What do you do to get what you want?
12. What kinds of satisfactions have you had?
13. Does anyone know who you really are?
14. What kinds of disappointments or difficulties have you had?
15. Do you feel that anyone really cares what happens to you?

Role Playing
and Role Reversals

Masks:
A Racial Role Reversal

Goal

To help group members identify racist attitudes in their own behavior.

Group Size

Unlimited.

Time Required

Approximately two hours.

Materials

    I. Two masks, one black and one white.

    II. Newsprint, a felt-tipped marker, and masking tape.

    III. Paper and pencils.

Physical Setting

A room large enough to accommodate all participants comfortably, with chairs placed in a large circle.

Submitted by John Lawton.

Process

I. The facilitator begins with a discussion on racism and the importance of identifying racist attitudes in one's own behavior. He explains that the activity is designed to make the participants more sensitive to their own attitudes and behavior toward other racial and ethnic groups in the community.

II. The facilitator chooses one black and one white participant to move to the center of the circle. The black member is given a white mask and the white member is given a black mask. Their task will be to switch roles and to discuss a current issue relating to race.

III. The facilitator selects another mixed dyad to act as "reality testers." Each one is to stand behind the masked participant of the opposite race and to indicate when that person acts out-of-role by tapping him on the shoulder. The reality tester should also jot down the reason for his move.

IV. The remaining participants are divided into two observer groups. One group will observe the masked dyad, the other group will observe the reality testers. Each time a tap is made, the observers are to write down what they think the out-of-role behavior was. The facilitator distributes pencils and paper to the observers and reality testers.

V. The facilitator asks the masked dyad to begin the dialog. After ten or fifteen minutes, he interrupts the discussion and divides the entire group into triads, allowing individual group members to verbalize their perceptions of statements checked by the reality testers. The subgroups are to list variations in perceptions for total group discussion.

VI. When the task is completed, the facilitator reassembles the group and appoints a recording secretary to list the subgroup reactions on newsprint. At this point, the group responds to variations in perceptions that were discovered at each check point (tap). When this is completed, the reality testers give their input in the order that checking took place.

VII. Participants form triads and attempt to identify from the data a list of their own perceptions on indications of racism.

VIII. The facilitator reassembles the total group and leads a discussion on the indications of racism that were identified. He may want to copy the list on newsprint. This list may be used to develop an agenda or goals for the future.

Listening-Confronting:
A Racial Role-Reversal Experience

Goals

I. To examine grievances resulting from racial attitudes by utilizing listening and paraphrasing techniques in a role-reversal situation.

II. To give participants, in a relatively safe and structured setting, the opportunity to send and receive messages that would be threatening in a "normal" situation.

Group Size

Ten to fifty participants.

Time Required

Two hours.

Materials

I. Pencils, newsprint, and felt-tipped markers.

II. A 5″ × 8″ index card for each participant.

III. A 2″ × 6″ slip of paper for each participant.

IV. Boxes from which to draw slips.

Physical Setting

A room large enough for the group to sit in a group-on-group arrangement; separate rooms to generate data.

Process

I. The facilitator separates the participants into two groups by race. Each group is instructed to appoint a *task master,* who has the responsibility of keeping the group on task and ensuring that the group adheres to its time commitments.

Submitted by Marvin Dunn, Robert Solomon, Tom Puroff, Miguel Gonzalez-Pando, and Robert Beneckson.

II. Each group is instructed to generate a list of the other group's behaviors that make it feel uneasy, afraid, alienated, angry, or in any way in conflict with that group:

1. Each group member is given a 5″ × 8″ index card and is instructed to write down incidents in which he has been involved or with which he is familiar that have resulted in negative feelings toward members of the other group.

2. The task master collects the cards and discusses the data with the group. The data from the individual cards are listed on newsprint, making a composite group list.

III. Each racial group transcribes the data from its composite list onto 2″ × 6″ slips for the role-playing session that is to follow. Because there must be one slip for each participant, some grievances may have to be repeated on several slips.

IV. After the completion of steps II and III, the total group reconvenes and the composite lists from each group are posted.

V. The facilitator divides the total group into two subgroups of equal size, ensuring that racial groups are represented proportionately in *each* group. He labels one group "white" and the other "minority." The members of the "white" group will wear cards labeled "white." Members of the "minority" group will wear cards labeled "minority." (If the group is very large, the facilitator may ask some members to form an outer circle to observe the role-interaction process of the inner group. If the group is small enough, everyone participates.)

VI. The grievance slips generated by the two racial groups in step III are placed in separate boxes, one labeled "grievances identified by whites," and the other "grievances identified by the minority." The members of the "white" group draw from the boxes labeled "grievances identified by whites," and members of the "minority" group draw from the box labeled "grievances identified by the minority." Each participant reads his slip and concentrates on placing himself in the role of the person for whom the grievance is *real*.

VII. Each member of the group communicates the grievance on his slip to a member of the other group. Example: If a member of the "white" group (John) drew a grievance slip that said, "It bothers me when I see minority persons eating lunch together with whites excluded from the table," he might address this message to any individual in the "minority" group: "Betty, it makes me feel upset and scared when I see minority persons eating lunch together without any whites." This form should be used in sending all messages: *the name of the person to whom the message is being sent;* "*it makes me feel,*" followed by *the feeling that is to be communicated;* and *the content of the message* itself.

VIII. The person who receives the message (Betty) then paraphrases and repeats it to the sender in the following manner: "John, I hear you saying that you feel very upset and frightened when you see members of a minority group eating by themselves." The paraphrased message takes the following form: *name of sender;* "*I hear you saying*"; the *feeling communicated* by the sender; and the *content of the message.* If the paraphrased message is satisfactory to the sender and to the facilitator, a new message is sent by another group member. This process continues until all messages from the first group are sent, received, and paraphrased correctly.

IX. Members of the other group now send their messages and hear them paraphrased in the same manner.

NOTE: It is important for the facilitator and the task masters to keep the group on task and maintain the structure of the communications as indicated earlier. Neither explanations nor defenses for the behaviors are allowed. This is an experience in listening and trying to understand messages.

The Trouble with David:
A Role Play in Three Acts

Goals

I. To encourage participants to communicate their emotions accurately to others.

II. To help participants observe their own and others' behavior and the interrelationships that exist between such behaviors.

III. To help illustrate and clarify stereotyped views of other racial groups.

Group Size

Unlimited.

Time Required

Approximately three hours.

Materials

I. A copy of The Trouble with David Background Sheet and a copy of The Trouble with David Role-Play Sheet for each participant.

II. A copy of the appropriate Role-Description Sheet for each role player.

III. A copy of The Trouble with David Observer's Guide for each observer.

Physical Setting

A room large enough for all participants to be seated comfortably.

Designed by Arthur M. Freedman. Jim Schultz is acknowledged for inspiring the activity and assisting in its initial implementation.

Process

I. The facilitator divides the participants into smaller discussion groups and distributes a copy of The Trouble with David Background Sheet to each participant.

II. The groups meet separately and discuss the situation presented, considering as many different points of view as possible: the child's, the other children's, the teacher's, the teacher's aide's, the child's mother, the social worker's, the program administrator's. Each group may select a recording secretary if it wishes.

III. The discussion groups disband, and the facilitator distributes a copy of The Trouble with David Role-Play Sheet to each participant and explains the role play.

IV. The facilitator selects five participants to play the major roles. The remaining participants are designated as observers. He gives each role player a copy of his appropriate Role-Description Sheet and each observer a copy of The Trouble with David Observer's Guide, and allows time for the material to be studied.

V. Act I of the role play begins, following the directions on The Trouble with David Role-Play Sheet.

VI. Between Act I and Act II, ten minutes is provided for each role player to share his feelings and expectations with the other players and with the observers. Each role player should consider whether he was communicating effectively with the other players; if he believes he was not being understood, he should indicate what behavior of the other person signalled this misunderstanding.

VII. The observers then share their observations.

VIII. Next, differences between the role players' views of what happened and the observers' views are explored.

IX. Acts II and III proceed in the same way as Act I.

X. The facilitator leads a discussion of the different ways that two involved people or groups may see the same event, focusing on the issues of how a person's *attitudes, values,* and *expectations* contribute to his *selective perceptions* of the observed interaction and of how people tend to *act* in ways that are consistent with their *perceptions.*

The Trouble with David Background Sheet

This situation concerns David, a four-year-old black boy who misbehaves at Head Start school, disrupting his entire class. He screams and shouts, cries, runs around the classroom, and generally behaves in a wild and uncontrolled manner.

Occasionally, he does become interested in an activity (though never of a group nature), but he always becomes distracted before he is finished and often ends by tearing up what he has done and throwing things around the room.

David's behavior obviously affects those around him: his mother, his teacher, the teacher's aide, and the social worker. The way in which the problem is resolved will have a great deal to do with the specific emotional impact of David's behavior on these people.

The Trouble with David Role-Play Sheet

Act I: *Players:* (1) teacher
(2) teacher's aide.

Time: 20 minutes.

Location: A conference room at the school.

Goal of Act I: To set up a meeting between David's mother and one of the staff if necessary.

Options: (1) The social worker may or may not be present or may be brought into the meeting at any time—it is entirely up to the teacher and the teacher's aide.

(2) The problem may or may not be dealt with at this point. More meetings with other people may be necessary—such as with David's mother, with David, or with the social worker. One or more of these people can meet with the social worker during Act II or Act III.

Act II: *Players:* (1) David's mother
(2) one of the school staff.

Time: 10 minutes.

Location: David's home.

Goal of Act II: What happens now depends upon what occurred in Act I.

Options: The players included here will have been determined in Act I; David may or may not be present.

Act III: *Players:* (1) teacher
(2) David.

Time: 20 minutes.

Location: The school classroom.

Goal of Act III: The problem must be resolved during this act.

Options: Any combination of players may be involved in this act in any sequence and for any portion of the act.

Role-Description Sheet: David

Your name is David. You are a four-year-old boy. This is your first week at Head Start school. Your mother told you that you had better be a good boy and not make any trouble or she would make sure that you would be sorry.

Because this is the first time you have ever been away from home and your brothers and sisters, you are *very* nervous and excited about being in these new surroundings. Your mother has told you that it is *very* important for you to be here with a lot of other children your age—which is also new for you—even if you don't know who they are or what you are supposed to do or what your mother meant when she warned you about getting into trouble—whatever "trouble" means.

Every day when you get to the school you come into a big room with a lot of children and two grown-up people. But you don't know who they are or what they are trying to do or what they want you to do. The grown-up lady with the white skin looks funny because you've never been with a person who has white skin before. She really is very strange with all the smiling she does all the time, even when nobody has done anything funny to make her laugh. You feel scared, and there she is smiling—you think that she must be happy *because* you're scared—maybe she *wants* you to feel scared. At home, when you got scared, you would cry and scream and run up and down the room until you got somebody's attention—even though you usually got a slap in the face or somebody hollering at you to shut up. At least that was better than being smiled at, because that doesn't make any sense at all. Why should a grown-up with white skin smile when all the grown-ups you know either yell at you or slap you when you start running around? When you're in this school and you act the way you do at home, all the other kids just look at you and move away from you, leaving you alone, and you don't like that *at all.* It is all very scary. Then after a while, the white lady comes over to you with a worried look on her funny face and she says, "What's the matter, David?" You can't answer her—she's so strange and scary-looking, and you never had a grown-up act like this with you before.

Maybe this is what your mother was talking about when she told you to stay out of trouble. That probably means you're really going to get a beating when your mother hears about this. That funny-looking grown-up lady—*she's* the one that's going to get *you* into trouble.

Role-Description Sheet: David's Mother

You are a black mother of seven children. You have not seen your husband for the past two years.

Yesterday you got a phone call from the people at David's school. David is your youngest child—and probably the wildest. They say he's been making trouble, and they want to come and talk with you about the disturbances. You don't understand why they are so upset. All you ever have to do when David gets wild is to yell at him or give him a good belt on the backside—that usually shuts him up. But anyhow, he's made some trouble for you, and you are angry with him. For four years you've been stuck around the house with him, but finally someone started this Head Start school. It was beginning to look as though you were going to have some peace and quiet during the summer. But now, because of the trouble he's started, they'll probably try to throw him out of the school. You'll be stuck with him again and won't be able to have any time for yourself. It's all David's fault.

You wonder what those people from the school are going to say, and you worry about what David might have done to get them so angry. What you've got to do is arrange it so that they don't throw him out of school. After all, a hot summer is bad enough without having to chase around after a child all day. But you can't say that to *that* kind of people. Maybe you'd better tell them how all your other kids had trouble in school because they were "deprived"—that's a good word; people like them like it. You could tell them that you don't want *this* kid to have the same kind of trouble that all the others did. If they throw him out of school, whatever happens will be *their* fault. Maybe that will help them feel sorry or guilty enough to let David stay in school this summer. Then maybe you'll be able to keep on enjoying yourself as you have been for the last week while David has been at school.

Role-Description Sheet: Teacher

You are a young, white woman who has been teaching for two years. David has been very upset since he started the summer Head Start program a week ago. You are not sure what is troubling him, and you cannot find any reasons to explain his behavior. He has the same background as all the other kids and *they* have not been behaving the way he has. David has been *so* wild that you have barely been able to control him. You are beginning to wonder just how much longer you will be able to do so. You would like to help, but you really do not know what to do. You are afraid that if you try anything else, it might be a mistake and only make things worse for David—and yourself. If you make a mistake, it would not look good at all—because you're supposed to be trained to handle such problems.

Also, your teacher's aide is becoming a problem, telling you that you ought to punish the child until he improves. You think that David will not learn by being punished because he just does not know any other way to act. But, even though you have tried, you just do not know *how* to teach him any other way of behaving in the schoolroom. You are sure that what he needs is someone with more skill and experience than you have to show him or to teach him another way of behaving. Maybe he needs some kind of therapy—after all, his behavior is *very* unusual.

You have decided that your only choice now is to ask the social worker to help you out. After all, she is supposed to be *the* expert in this kind of thing. But it is *very* important that she does not do *too* good a job *too* fast, because then it would look as if you were not able to do your job at all.

You think it might be a good idea to talk the problem over once more with your teacher's aide to see if the two of you can figure out a solution without calling on the social worker.

Role-Description Sheet: Teacher's Aide

You are a black high-school student who is working as a teacher's aide for the Head Start program this summer. One of the kids has been disruptive since he started in school about a week ago. The white teacher you have been working with seems to be unsure about what to do with David. She has been asking him what is bothering him, but he just looks at her and gets wide-eyed and behaves worse than ever. What he needs is a good swift belt in the pants—but everyone tells you that you cannot do anything like that in Head Start school. But what else is there to do? You suppose you could probably put him in a corner, but you cannot figure out what good that would do. Besides, the teacher does not seem to like that idea either. Every time you tell her she ought to punish him, she says, "No"—but she never does anything else that works. You are beginning to wonder if she knows anything at all about what she is supposed to do in a case like this.

Role-Description Sheet: Social Worker

You are a middle-aged, white social worker with a master's degree. You have heard through the grapevine that the new young teacher has been having some trouble with one of the children. You do not know very much about the teacher, but you would not be surprised to get a request for advice or help. You are not sure what the problem is, but you have an idea that the teacher is unsure of herself and that the child might be getting even more confused and upset because the teacher does not know what to do and may be acting erratically and inconsistently.

Before you can do anything—and you really *would* like to help if you can—you have to be *invited* first, since it would not be acceptable just to walk in and take over. But if you *are* invited, the first thing you will have to do will be to get all the facts from the teacher, her aide, and then the child. If you cannot help them solve the problem or solve it yourself, you might have to see the child's parents—*both* of them. If nothing seems to work out, you know that you will have to request that the child be withdrawn from the program. Although you would like to see *every* child helped, the Head Start program has enough problems without having to spend so much time and energy on just one child. Time spent on one disruptive child can be used more productively with other children who are better adjusted. So, for you, the question is how much effort you are willing to expend—you may have to decide if it is worth it for a social worker, a teacher, and a teacher's aide to spend so much time and trouble to try to help *one* child.

You do not know the answer to that question—but you are painfully aware that it may have to be asked—and answered.

The Trouble with David Observer's Guide

You are to function as an observer during the role play to follow.

During the role play:

1. Focus on the *manner* in which the players are interacting—who was most (or least) actively participating; who was most (or least) influential in the interactions; and the *feelings* the players are (or are *not*) expressing. Do not be concerned about their *remarks* concerning "the trouble with David."

2. Be prepared to report on specific incidents or examples of each player's behavior and the reactions and expressed feelings that his behavior evoked from the other players.

After each act:

1. Encourage the players to discuss their own behavior and feelings —try to *draw them out* by asking open-ended questions until you are able to understand clearly what *concerned* them during the role play. This is important because it is their concerns that will have influenced the way they behaved.

2. Give the players a chance to explain *their* understanding of what happened.

3. Share with the players *your* understanding of what happened. In doing this, be sure to include a description of the specific behavior of the players involved that led you to your conclusions.

4. Check with the role players to make sure that they *understand* what you are trying to communicate to them. One way to do this might be to ask them to repeat in their own words what you have just said before they respond to your observation.

5. Finally, invite the players to join with you in identifying the *differences* between their observations and yours. It is important to examine those differences in order to understand how two groups can see the *same* event in very different ways.

Structured Experiences:
Intergroup

Albatross:
An Activity in Differing Values

Goals

    I. To increase participants' awareness of phenomena that occur between groups with different value systems.

    II. To involve participants in a simulated society in which they encounter persons very different from themselves.

Group Size

Unlimited.

Time Required

Approximately one hour.

Materials

    I. A copy of the Albatross Role-Description Sheet for each role player.

    II. Newsprint and a felt-tipped marker.

Physical Setting

Two rooms, each large enough to accommodate all participants comfortably.

Submitted by Susan Ells.

Process

I. The facilitator chooses two persons, one female and one male, to act in a role play involving a simulated culture. Each role player is given a copy of the Albatross Role-Description Sheet to prepare for the role play. The facilitator emphasizes that the role-playing activity is to be nonverbal, that the role players are to express themselves in actions, not words. The role players go into another room.

II. He then asks for six to eight volunteers to be "guests" in the role play.

III. The facilitator discusses the role play with the remaining participants, who are designated as observers. He indicates that the situation will be as follows: "You are about to be involved in an activity concerning cultural norms and values. When you walk into the next room, you will be entering a new culture —the culture of Albatross. You are a guest in this new culture. Because this is a *nonverbal* activity, please do not talk after entering the Albatrossian culture." The facilitator answers any questions they may have. (Ten minutes.)

IV. The observers are directed to the other room, and the role play begins.

V. After the nonverbal role play has ended, the observers, as a group, take ten minutes to list various cultural traits that they think were demonstrated during the role play. The facilitator lists these traits on newsprint. Then the role players explain, in Albatrossian terms, each trait the group listed correctly.

VI. Finally, the facilitator leads the total group in a discussion about the misunderstandings that occur between groups with different value systems. Depending on the interests of the participants, the discussion may include black-white, male-female, Arab-Israeli, or teacher-student value systems. Individual ethnocentrism and feelings of trust, empathy, disgust, hostility, and fear can also be discussed.

Albatross Role-Description Sheet

You live in a subculture called Albatross. The Albatrossian culture is viewed as counter-American because each custom is either physically or intellectually opposed to traditional, middle-class American customs or ways of thinking. The following are two examples of Albatrossian customs as explained in Albatrossian terms:

1. When greeting a guest, the Albatrossian removes that person's right shoe and briefly massages the foot. Even though the right foot, in the Albatrossian view, is not considered more important than the left foot, people in Albatross tend to use their right foot more. In other words, the Albatrossians do not believe (as opposed to the dominant American view) that there must be a reason for every important custom.

2. Being second in the Albatrossian culture is more important than being first because Albatrossians view the natural world as full of dangers and fears. Hence, to be served second or to be greeted second is to be protected from potential dangers (poisoned food, an unknown enemy). Thus, males are always greeted and served first; females are served last.

This is a *nonverbal* activity. You are to illustrate Albatrossian customs in *all* your actions, including greeting your guests.

Central University:
Managing Intergroup Conflict

Goals

    I. To identify and manage intergroup conflict.

    II. To illustrate intervention strategies during a crisis.

    III. To demonstrate the dynamics of the negotiation process.

Group Size

From nine to thirty-six participants. Additional persons may be assigned observer roles.

Time Required

At least four hours.

Materials

    I. A copy of the Central University Diagram for each participant.

    II. A copy of the Central University Student Letter for each member of the administration, faculty, student, and consultant subgroups.

    III. A copy of the appropriate Role-Description Sheet for each member of the administration, faculty, student, and consultant subgroups.

Physical Setting

A room large enough for the four subgroups to meet separately.

Process

    I. The facilitator gives an overview of the activity.

    II. He instructs participants to line up in a continuum ranging from conservative to radical. (The lineup is to be accomplished nonverbally.)

Developed by Arthur M. Freedman, with Charles Hamilton, Howard Williams, George Taylor, and Michael Klaber.

III. The continuum is divided into thirds as follows:
1. Administrators (conservatives)
2. Faculty members (middle-of-the-road)
    a. one-third pro-administration
    b. one-third pro-student
    c. one-third neutral
3. Students (radicals).

IV. The facilitator distributes copies of the Central University Diagram and the Central University Student Letter to participants. Then he distributes appropriate role-description sheets to the subgroups.

V. Each of the subgroups selects (a) one of its members to become part of a three-man consultant team (this team assembles immediately to begin its strategy); (b) one person to act as its representative at the negotiations; and (c) another person to act as the internal coordinator of the group. The latter two may be the same person, and these roles can be changed at any time.

VI. Up to five rounds are conducted. Each round consists of one thirty-minute period during which each group, separately, plans strategy for its intergroup negotiations (and/or evaluates its most current negotiations), and one ten-minute period during which the representatives of each group meet in a group-on-group design for negotiations. Thus, a round consists of:
a. Strategy planning and/or evaluation—thirty minutes.
b. Negotiations among representatives in a group-on-group design—ten minutes.

VII. Prior to the discussion, the facilitator asks participants to complete the following statements (in sequence):
1. "I have learned . . ." (theory building)
2. "As I *now* reflect on my real-life situation, I remind myself that . . ." (application)
3. "When I return to my back-home situation, I will . . ." (commitment to action).

VIII. The facilitator leads a discussion of the activity.

Central University Diagram

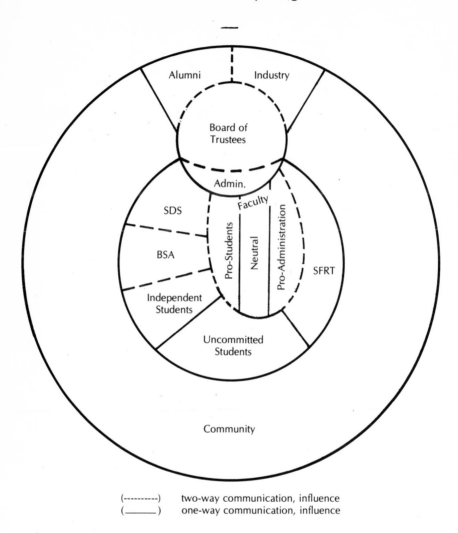

(----------)   two-way communication, influence
(_____)   one-way communication, influence

SDS—Students for a Democratic Society

BSA—Black Students Association

SFRT—Students Favoring the Restoration of Tradition

Central University Student Letter

FROM: The Coalition of Socially Concerned and Socially Aware Students

TO: The Board of Directors, Administration, and Faculty of Central University.

We, the undersigned Coalition of Socially Concerned and Socially Aware Students of this University, in pursuit of the discharge of our felt moral imperatives, are herewith presenting a list of ten demands. We expect that your rapid acceptance of these demands will eliminate the sources of your traditional and systematic suppression of students' inalienable rights to actively participate in the process of their own education.

We demand that these ten points be considered AND acted on by the total university establishment by the end of five negotiation sessions. Should a mutually satisfactory and BINDING agreement on these ten points NOT be achieved by that time, it should be expected that the physical EXISTENCE of the university will be endangered.

1. A black studies program, satisfactory to the Black Students Association, shall be developed and instituted.
2. Students shall be allowed to participate in hiring faculty and in faculty firing standards and procedures.
3. Scholarship monies shall be made available for the purpose of recruiting students from racial and ethnic minorities from whom the advantages of a university education have been systematically withheld.
4. Separate housing and social center facilities shall be made available to all black students.
5. The university ROTC program shall be terminated.
6. Students already suspended shall (a) be reinstated and (b) not be held responsible for damage to university property.
7. The university shall actively provide support, in the form of housing subsidies, for the surrounding ghetto communities.
8. A course in white racism shall be developed and instituted; it shall include consideration of institutional racism, and it shall be a required undergraduate course.
9. The university shall discontinue work on any projects funded by monies provided by any agency working for or associated

with the Armed Services; further, no such grants shall be accepted in the future.

10. All future construction on campus shall be done with labor that includes a minimum of 40 percent black laborers and 20 percent black foremen.

(Signed)

Coalition of Socially Concerned and Socially Aware Students:
    300 BSA students
     80 SDS students
     25 independent dissenting students

Role-Description Sheet: Administration

You are a member of a small group of administrators who have been selected by your peers to represent their interests during the forthcoming negotiations with dissenting university students. One of you is the special administrative assistant to the university president and has the president's OK to take action if and when necessary to maintain order; but there are no guidelines as to what concessions, if any, might be acceptable either to the president or to the board of trustees. However, it is obviously necessary to maintain the approval of the board because it controls the budgets for a number of projects in which all of you have some direct or indirect investment. The other members of this group are department heads, divisional deans, or student personnel administrators. Thus, you are all highly placed, highly respected people with many years of experiencing full control over the behaviors of those whose positions are lower than your own, such as faculty, staff members, and students.

You are very satisfied with your experiences within the university and with the way the board has always established reasonable policies and practices governing university life. Your experience has been that periodic disturbances can be tolerated until they blow over, as long as the existing rules are adhered to and dissent from below is listened to but not acted on. As one of the members of the board said the other evening over cocktails, "Students come and go, but the university will exist forever."

In general, the attitude of the administrators and the board of trustees is to reject nothing, accept nothing, stall for time (if possible), and wait until the agitators get tired, give up, and go home. This expectation is reasonable, because no other group of students at Central University has ever succeeded in going further.

Role-Description Sheet: Faculty

You are a member of a small group of faculty members who have been selected by your peers to represent their respective interests during the forthcoming negotiations with dissenting students. You range in rank from instructors to full professors. None of you hold administrative positions.

There is considerable disagreement among your group concerning the present crisis. Three different subgroups exist:

1. Those of you who are fully committed to the conservative position assumed by the administration and the board of trustees. You do not intend to allow naive and misguided student rabble to disturb the university—an institution that represents the culmination of the efforts of generations of dedicated academicians who have worked to discover, accumulate, and disseminate knowledge. You believe that students have no right to dictate the terms of their education because they cannot have developed any meaningful criteria to determine which subjects might be relevant for their education in a world about which they know very little, if anything.

2. Those of you who believe that the students are in the very best position to determine what is and what is not relevant to them. You are inclined to support the dissenting students very strongly because you believe that people who are affected by decisions are entitled to participate in the making of those decisions.

3. Those of you who are not committed to either of these positions. Instead, you are very strongly committed to the early resolution of the present crisis; whatever its form, the business of education must continue. Besides, constant stress like this is bad for one's digestion.

Role-Description Sheet: Students

You are a member of the Coalition of Socially Concerned and Socially Aware Students, which consists of the Black Students Association, Students for a Democratic Society, and independent students. You have been selected by your peers to represent their interests during the forthcoming confrontations with the establishment. You represent slightly less than 20 percent of the total student body.

In spite of a small but noisy conservative backlash element (about 12 percent of the total student body), you believe that most of the students at Central University agree with most, if not all, of your ten demands. This support, however, has been voiced mostly in private rather than where it would be most helpful—that is, in public print (such as the signatures of the 405 students on the list of demands). However, you expect that when you successfully complete your confrontations, those presently uncommitted will openly join forces with your coalition. Of course, you will probably continue to have trouble with conservative elements such as the SFRT (Students Favoring the Restoration of Tradition) and a sizeable group of faculty. You expect opposition because you have come to realize that old beliefs die hard and that it is often necessary to facilitate the passing of anachronistic beliefs through a rigorously applied program of dissent and confrontation.

Role-Description Sheet: Consultants

You are members of a three-person group of local consultants who are concerned with the present crisis at Central University. Although no one at Central University explicitly requested your assistance, the three of you are highly motivated to do whatever you can to resolve any conflict before violence occurs.

Your task is to develop an entry strategy within the limits dictated by your group's values.

Acme General Service Company: A Multiple Role Play

Goal

    I. To increase awareness of racist feelings.

    II. To help eliminate racist attitudes.

Group Size

An unlimited number of groups of four participants each.

Time Required

Approximately one hour.

Materials

    I. A copy of the Acme General Service Company Information Sheet for each participant.

    II. A copy of the appropriate Acme General Service Company Role-Description Sheet for each role player.

    III. Two black masks and two white masks for each subgroup.

Process

    I. The facilitator divides the participants into subgroups of four members each.

    II. He distributes a copy of the Acme General Service Company Information Sheet to each participant.

    III. He then assigns a role to each participant and gives each role player his appropriate Role-Description Sheet and an appropriate mask. The role players are given ten minutes to study their own role descriptions.

    IV. The role play is acted out within each of the subgroups simultaneously. (Twenty minutes.)

Submitted by Arthur M. Freedman.

V. Each subgroup discusses the racist feelings generated during the role play. The subgroups are given the task of developing at least one generalization about the relationship between racism and communication.

VI. The facilitator reassembles the entire group, calls for reports from each of the subgroups, and leads a discussion of the entire experience.

VII. If time permits, the facilitator may wish to provide participants with an opportunity to commit themselves to *do* something when they return to their work situations (participants complete the statement, "When I return to work, I will . . .").

Acme General Service Company Information Sheet

You are a member of a four-person work group whose job is to provide a wide variety of specialized services to customers.

Two members of your group are supervisors and two are assistants. Each of you is able to do the jobs of the other three. However, the two supervisors have had a great deal of experience, and they are the only people in your work group who communicate with the departmental director.

Within your department there are two other four-person work groups that do the same kind of work as your group. The company always promotes its own people when someone at a higher position in the organization's structure retires, dies, or leaves the company. Promotion is determined by the following factors: (1) the length of time a person has been employed by the company; (2) the person's reliability (that is, few absences from the job for illness or any other reason, few major errors in doing his job); and (3) evidence of initiative and creativity (that is, the individual's contribution to increase the company's efficiency and/or reduce the company's costs through useful suggestions). The company does not consider a person's race, religion, sex, or political affiliation in making its decisions about promotions, particularly since the affirmative-action legislation was passed.

Several weeks ago, your group heard that a supervisor's job was opening in one of the other four-man work groups in your department. Both of the assistants in your work group are next in line for promotion. Compared with the other assistants in the department, they have been with the company longer, have been more reliable, and have contributed more frequently to the company's efficiency. Neither of the two supervisors in your work group is personally interested in the new job opening. The decision will be made by the director of the department.

Until now, your group has worked together very well. Everyone did his job and there has seldom been any friction among you. However, since the news about the new job opening, many mistakes have been made, and all the members of your work group—particularly the two assistants—have begun to accuse each other of being responsible for the mistakes.

The director of your department has noticed these errors and the hard feelings in your group. He has told each of you that he knows you have not had any problems like this before and that you should all sit down together and decide (1) what went wrong, and (2) what problem exists among the four of you.

Today your group is meeting to discuss the agenda established by the director.

Acme General Service Company Role-Description Sheets

Player Number 1

You are a black supervisor who, together with another supervisor (white) and two assistants (one white and one black), works in a four-man group.

You have worked quite hard to reach your present position, which has enabled you to obtain a great number of social and economic advantages that you would not have been able to enjoy otherwise. You are, therefore, devoted to doing your job as well as you possibly can.

You are not particularly concerned with anyone else's personal problems. Nor do you worry about competition with others, because you feel that if everyone—including yourself—does his own job, he will or will not advance on the basis of his performance. You feel that while at work, each worker should be most concerned about his own job.

You are particularly careful *not* to show any signs of special preference or help toward other blacks because you do not want your department's director to think you are prejudiced against whites: first, because you believe that this is not true, and second, because you are afraid that it would give him a bad impression of blacks in general.

Player Number 2

You are a white supervisor who, together with another supervisor (black) and two assistants (one white and one black), works in a four-man group. The company has forced you to work with blacks. You believe that blacks are not capable of doing as good a job as whites—blacks are not trustworthy and they watch out for each other too much. If blacks get a chance, you believe they will work together to *prevent* a white person from getting the promotion to which he is entitled.

You think it is only right and proper that whites should supervise blacks and that blacks should never be allowed to supervise whites. You are afraid that the black supervisor with whom you work is teaming up with the black assistant to prevent the white assistant from getting a promotion by making him look bad to the director of the department.

Player Number 3

You are a white assistant who, along with a black assistant, works under the direction of one black and one white supervisor in a four-man group. You have worked long and hard to master your department's work, and you intend to show the director that you are the most capable assistant in the department. You think that you are most qualified to be promoted to the position of supervisor because of your excellent past performance. However, you also know that the other assistant in your group is a very good worker and that he has just as good a chance of being promoted as you do. You believe that the director of the department is fair and that he will promote the person who can do the best job. You think that a person should be considered for promotion *only* on the basis of the quality of his work; you would resent it if you were promoted for any other reason.

Player Number 4

You are a black assistant who, along with a white assistant, works under the direction of one black and one white supervisor in a four-man group. You know that you and the white assistant are both in line for the next promotion.

You are afraid that the other assistant and the white supervisor have teamed up to make you look bad to the department director. You believe that if only you could get the black supervisor to take your part, the two of you might be able to overcome the white team. However, in all the time you have worked with the man, he has never given you any reason to think he would do this for you or anyone else. You believe that this is *wrong*—it is almost like being *cheated*. After all, you *are* both blacks and blacks *should* stick together and help each other.

And, although you would never admit it to anyone else (in fact, you do not even like to admit it to yourself), you *do* feel that you really *need* help. But you do not want it to *look* as though you need help *because* you are black.

Even though both your supervisors have at one time or another told you that your work is excellent, you are afraid that it really does not compete with the white assistant's work. But you also feel this may be because he has been getting help from the white supervisor while you have received *no* help from the black supervisor. This is *just not fair!*

Community Crisis: Intergroup Problem Solving

Goals

 I. To gain skill in determining, stating, and solving community-related problems.

 II. To develop the ability to work together on a problem despite conflicting group interests.

Group Size

An unlimited number of participants, divided into four groups.

Time Required

Approximately three hours. (May be divided into two sessions: problem identification and problem solving.)

Materials

 I. A copy of the Community Crisis Problem Sheet for each participant.

 II. A copy of the Community Crisis Tally Sheet for each group.

 III. For each group, ten copies of the appropriate Community Crisis Ballot Sheet.

 IV. A copy of the Community Crisis Representative Briefing Sheet for each group representative.

 V. Paper "money": $500,000 in denominations of $1,000, $5,000, and $10,000.

 VI. Pencils.

Submitted by Arthur M. Freedman.
 This structured experience was originally entitled "The Critical Situation," written by David Popoff, and published in *Psychology Today* in 1968. A subsequent version was adapted by Arthur M. Freedman from materials prepared by the staff of the Behavioral Science Center (BSC) of Sterling Institute, including James Barton, Jesse Borjorquez, John Hayes, and Percy Wilson. BSC also acknowledges the contribution of Irwin Rubin of the Sloan School of Management, Massachusetts Institute of Technology.

Physical Setting

A room large enough for each group to meet separately, and a table at which to seat the representatives of the four groups.

Process

    I. The facilitator explains the goals of the structured experience.

    II. He distributes copies of the Community Crisis Problem Sheet to all participants, and participants read the information silently. (Five minutes.)

    III. Four equal-sized groups are formed and seated separately. The facilitator announces that the first task of each group is to define a problem according to the criteria given in the Community Crisis Problem Sheet. (Ten minutes.)

    IV. Then the facilitator directs the four groups to select *one* of the four crisis problems on which they can work together. (Fifteen minutes.)

    V. The facilitator designates each group to be one of the following community groups: business people, public officials, poor people, or militants. He distributes a copy of the Community Crisis Tally Sheet and the designated initial funds to each group. The voting options and procedures of the four groups are explained; because, in most communities, the power to make important decisions is distributed unevenly, the votes carry different weights.

        Groups are informed that they can *win* by solving the crisis problem. To do this, they need to make money according to the rules on the tally sheet. This money will represent whatever is meaningful for a given group, such as jobs, customers, sales, profits, houses, roads, taxes, education, health services, training, garbage collection, sewers, wells, transportation, land, and many other things. Just as important (and perhaps more so), money can also stand for the ability of the group to serve its interests and to benefit the community.

    VI. The facilitator announces that each group is to elect a representative who will cast the group's votes. (Groups may elect a new representative at any time except during negotiation and voting phases.)

VII. The facilitator distributes a set of the appropriate Community Crisis Ballot Sheet and a copy of the Community Crisis Representative Briefing Sheet to each elected representative. Each representative reads the briefing sheet aloud and discusses it with his "constituency." (Ten minutes.)

VIII. The facilitator explains that the payoff will be determined by the pattern of votes in each round and that he will announce which groups win and how much they win. He reminds the groups that they can win money *from* each other or lose money *to* each other.

IX. The facilitator announces the beginning of the five-minute voting period for round 1.

X. When the representatives have delivered their votes to the facilitator (they are allowed no more than five minutes), he tallies the votes on a chart like the following. (The vote for any group that either does not vote on time or does not vote at all will be considered a "no cooperation" vote.)

Round	Business People	Public Officials	Poor People	Militants	Voting Pattern
1					
2					
3					
4					
5					
6					
7					
8					
9					
10					

The facilitator reads the ballots aloud, determines the voting pattern, and announces the exchange of money according to the following schedule:

Voting Pattern	Results
Total of 0	*Riot.* Each group suffers a loss of half of its existing capital.
Total of 1, 2, or 5	*Special tax increase.* Public officials collect a tax of 10 percent of each group's capital, to cover the cost of increased police protection.
Total of 3	*Business backlash.* Business people cancel credit and collect $2,000 from each of the other groups.
Total of 4	*Militants prosper* and collect $5,000 from each of the other groups.
Total of 6 or 7	*Situation improves because of cooperative action.* Groups make gains according to how many times a cooperative total (6 or 7) has occurred, as in the following schedule.

	Business People	Public Officials	Poor People	Militants
First time	$30,000	$20,000	$10,000	$ 5,000
Second time	$20,000	$10,000	$20,000	$10,000
Third time	$10,000	$10,000	$30,000	$20,000
Fourth and subsequent times	$50,000	$40,000	$40,000	$30,000

"Police action," plus a total of 0 to 5.	*Unnecessary use of force.* Public officials suffer a loss of $5,000.
"Police action," plus a total of 6.	*Progress delayed.* Each group suffers a loss of $2,000.
One vote of "use force," plus a total of 0 to 3.	*Riot.* Each group loses half of its existing capital.
Two votes of "use force," plus any combination of other votes.	*Riot.* Each group loses half of its existing capital.

One vote of "use force," plus a total of 4 to 6.	*Progress delayed.* Each group suffers a loss of $2,000.
One vote of "use force," plus "police action," plus any combination of other votes.	Facilitators determine results by adding up the numbered votes.
Five consecutive votes resulting in a riot.	*Martial law.* Each group loses all its capital.

XI. The facilitator repeats step X for round 2 and round 3.

XII. After announcing the results for round 3, the facilitator directs the representatives to have a five-minute public meeting in the center of the room. (Only representatives may speak during this meeting.)

XIII. Step X is repeated for rounds 4, 5, and 6, followed by a second public meeting of representatives (as in step XII).

XIV. Step X is repeated for rounds 7, 8, and 9 (if martial law has not been declared), followed by the final mandatory public meeting of the representatives.

XV. Step X is repeated for round 10.

XVI. The facilitator calls for the final balances of the four groups, posting each on newsprint.

XVII. The groups meet separately to discuss the following three topics:
1. "I have learned . . ." (theory building)
2. "As I *now* think about what is going on in my own community, I remind myself that . . ." (application)
3. "When I return to my community, I will . . ." (commitment to action).

XVIII. The facilitator leads a general discussion of the experience, focusing on the relationships between cooperative action and conflicting group interests.

Community Crisis Problem Sheet

You will soon have the opportunity to form and test plans for solving real and important community problems.

By taking advantage of this opportunity, you can gain practice and skill in forming and carrying out such plans to solve important problems in your own community.

The Community Groups

You will become a member of one of four community groups:

- business people
- public officials (both elected and appointed)
- poor people
- militants.

Once you have become a member of a group, you will make plans, state positions, and take actions to solve an important problem from your group's point of view. But first you must choose the important problem that all different groups will seek to solve—a problem that is the cause of the critical community situation.

Choosing the Problem

The following suggestions should help you choose the kind of problem that will enable you to gain the greatest skill and practice in solving community problems. You will have thirty minutes to choose a problem.

Choose a *specific* problem, rather than a general problem. For example, "There aren't enough jobs" is a general problem; "The XYZ factory may close down" is a specific problem.

In addition, choose a specific problem that has caused a *critical community situation* to exist. This situation is critical because the community's business people, public officials, poor people, and militants must act quickly to solve the problem. If they do not, the critical community situation will get worse, and the result will probably be a *disaster.*

Choose a problem and a critical situation that could *actually* occur in your county, or in a similar community, and one on which business people, public officials, poor people, and militants *can work together* to solve. In other words, choose a problem that has resulted in a *critical* situation, but not in a situation where things have gone so far that no one can do anything about it.

Choose a problem that one or more of the community groups (i.e., business people, public officials, poor people, and militants) is *actively interested* in solving. Ideally, *all* groups should have an active interest in the problem.

Finally, choose a critical situation in which all groups can cooperate to solve the problem, but also one in which one or more groups stand to benefit (by obtaining more *money, power, prestige,* or other things they consider important) *at the expense* of one or more of the other groups by *refusing to cooperate* with them or by acting against them.

Example of a Critical Situation

The following problem was selected by participants in a community-development workshop.

> New regulations made by the state will reduce welfare payments by the state government. In the community, the governments of the town and the county must decide whether to make additional welfare payments of their own so that the community's welfare recipients will not suffer any loss of income when the state's new regulations go into effect. But the town has made political commitments *not* to raise taxes. And, meanwhile, the Public Housing Agency (a state agency) is expanding and raising its rents.

Review

In describing your problem and your critical situation, you should be able to answer "yes" to the following questions. Have you chosen:

- a *critical situation* that has arisen because of a *specific* problem?
- a situation that is likely to get worse and result in a *disaster,* unless the four community groups act quickly?
- a problem and a critical situation that could *actually occur* in your community?
- a problem that the four community groups (business people, public officials, poor people, and militants) *can work together* to solve?
- a problem that one or more of the community groups want very much to solve?
- a critical situation in which one or more of the community groups stand to benefit at the *expense* of one or more of the other groups, by refusing to cooperate with them or by attacking them?

Community Crisis Representative Briefing Sheet

You have the power to vote for your group. You may receive instructions from your goup to cast a specific vote, or you may receive instructions to vote as you think best.

You are responsible to your group. Groups may select a new representative at any time, except during negotiations and voting.

Voting Process

You will cast your votes on the ballots provided for your group. Write a brief description of the reasons for your vote in the space provided on the ballot. These descriptions should be very brief, but they should also be specific. For example, the business person might vote "zero" because he believes that "the public officials can handle things." Or the militants might vote to "use force" because "that's the only way we can get people to listen to us."

When you cast a "cooperation" vote, write on the ballot a brief description of the cooperative action your group is prepared to take. For example, the public officials might "agree to a public meeting with representatives of the poor people." The poor people might be willing to "join the business people in lobbying for a highway."

When the poor people or the militants vote to "use force," their representative will write a brief description of the type of force they intend to use.

You may hold discussions with other representatives at any time to make deals or other arrangements. Group representatives *must* meet together after rounds 3, 6, and 9.

Community Crisis Ballot Sheet #1: Business People

Vote No. _____

Please vote on the action that you have chosen to take by circling one of the three alternatives below.

0   1   3

Briefly describe your reasons for choosing this action.

If you voted *3*, briefly describe a *specific* cooperative action that you are prepared to take.

Community Crisis Ballot Sheet #2: Public Officials

Vote No. _____

Please vote on the action that you have chosen to take by circling one of the three alternatives below.

Police Action   0   1

Briefly describe your reasons for choosing this action.

If you voted *1*, briefly describe a *specific* cooperative action that you are prepared to take.

Community Crisis Ballot Sheet #3: Poor People

Vote No. _____

Please vote on the action that you have chosen to take by circling one of the three alternatives below.

Use Force   0   2

Briefly describe your reasons for taking this action.

If you voted to *use force,* briefly describe what type of force you will use.

If you voted 2, briefly describe a *specific* cooperative action that you are prepared to take.

Community Crisis Ballot Sheet #4: Militants

Vote No. _____

Please vote on the action that you have chosen to take by circling one of the three alternatives below.

Use Force   0   1

Briefly describe your reasons for taking this action.

If you voted to *use force*, briefly describe what type of force you will use.

If you voted *1*, briefly describe a *specific* cooperative action that you are prepared to take.

Community Crisis Tally Sheet

Voting Options

Group	No Cooperation	Limited Cooperation	Cooperation	Initial Funds
Business People	0	1	3	$50,000
Public Officials	"Police Action"	0	1	$30,000
Poor People	"Use of Force"	0	2	$10,000
Militants	"Use of Force"	0	1	$ 5,000

Each voting round will take a maximum of five minutes. A failure to vote or a late vote by the poor people or the militants will be counted as a vote to use force. A failure to vote or a late vote by the business people will be counted as a vote of zero. And a failure to vote or a late vote by public officials will be counted as police action.

There are three ways to make money: gains, payoffs, and deals. Groups make *gains* when they cooperate with one another to help solve the problem that has resulted in the critical situation and to resolve the critical situation itself. Groups can make *deals* among themselves, using money to try to influence each other's actions. Groups can also make *payoffs* to each other, for taking actions that they have previously agreed upon.

Groups can also *lose* money. For example, because of the actions of all the groups, one group may be entitled to collect money from the other groups. In addition, if the groups fail to cooperate to solve the problem, then the critical situation may get worse, and any or all of the groups may suffer losses. The effect of a loss by any group is to reduce the sum of money available to that group. However, that group's loss does *not* increase the amount of money available to any other group.

Groups may run out of money. However, running out of money does *not* force a group to quit. A group that runs out of money can borrow money from other groups, make deals with other groups and collect payoffs, and continue to seek and make gains.

The effect of a gain by any group is to increase the amount of money available to that group. But that group's gain does *not* result in any reduction in the sum of money available to any other group.

There is enough money available to all groups to cover all gains that they can make.

Round	Your Group's Vote	Total Voting Result	Your Group's Payoff	Your Group's Balance
1			$	$
2				
3*				
4				
5				
6*				
7				
8				
9*				
10				

*Mandatory five-minute public meeting of representatives following this round, before the timing of the following round begins.

Community Construction:
An Unequal-Resource Activity

Goals

    I. To allow participants to act out their feelings about the processes involved when various ethnic groups acquire and utilize community resources.

    II. To increase the level of awareness and sensitivity to the kinds of pressures imposed by in-group members on out-group members.

    III. To experience what it feels like to be a member of another ethnic group.

    IV. To examine the various effects of institutional racism on members of different ethnic groups.

    V. To examine the consequences of entrapment in competitive situations that may lead to win-lose confrontations.

Group Size

A minimum of ten participants.

Time Required

Approximately three hours.

Materials

    I. Four hundred 5" x 8" index cards; four rolls of one-half-inch masking tape.

    II. Five felt-tipped markers.

    III. $1,000,000 in play money (or proportionate amounts as described below).

    IV. Newsprint.

Submitted by Marvin Dunn, Robert Solomon, Tom Puroff, Miguel Gonzalez-Pando, and Robert Beneckson.

Physical Setting

Preferably a carpeted room large enough to accommodate participants who will be working on the floor.

Process

I. Before the activity begins, the facilitator uses masking tape to divide the room into three separate areas, with one-half of the total area allocated to "whites," one-fourth to "blacks," and one-fourth to "Latins," or another ethnic group.

II. The facilitator forms three groups of approximately equal size. These groups are designated "White," "Black," and "Latin," and are assigned to designated areas. (All participants except designated representatives *must* remain in their assigned area.) Ethnic group designation cards are labeled. Each participant wears an index card (using masking tape). All cards for "whites" should be so labeled. Labels for members of other groups should reflect commonly used derogatory terms ("nigger," "colored," "jungle bunny," "wetback," "spic," etc.).

III. Resources, including index cards and play money, are distributed. Resources are allocated as follows:

	Cards	*Play* *Money*	*Rolls of* *Tape*
"Whites"	200	$200,000	2
"Blacks"	100	$100,000	1
"Latins"	100	$100,000	1

IV. The facilitator announces that each group will have one hour to build a community, using the materials supplied. Each group must decide *what* buildings it wants to construct and must purchase a building permit for each structure. Only one designated representative from each group may buy building permits. The facilitator also announces that he will determine the winning community on the basis of size, durability, and aesthetic appeal.

V. Prices for building permits are posted. Each group must purchase permits from the facilitator prior to building structures in its community. The price list:

Apartment buildings or common dwellings $10,000.00
Schools   5,000.00

Churches	2,500.00
Business establishments	5,000.00
Parks	5,000.00
Places of entertainment	5,000.00
Hospitals	7,500.00

Other community structures may be built if permits are approved and purchased from the building permit seller.

VI. The facilitator directs the three groups to designate one representative each.

VII. An enforcer (a member of the majority group who is selected to play that role) is chosen. He is to ensure that participants remain in their designated areas; he is also to act in an overtly oppressive manner toward minority-group members. The facilitator privately instructs him to prevent minority-group members from organizing against the system. The enforcer should side with the whites during any intergroup disputes or altercations.

VIII. A building permit seller (a member of the "White" group) is designated. The facilitator privately instructs him to discriminate covertly (i.e., grant whites building permits for less than the fee specified, while overcharging minority-group members).

IX. The building proceeds for thirty minutes, or until minority-group members rebel.

X. The facilitator announces which group has won the design/construction competition.

XI. The facilitator instructs groups to meet independently to discuss their reactions to the experience. (Ten minutes.)

XII. The representatives are assembled in a circle of six chairs in the center of the room. The facilitator joins them, and two empty chairs are made available for other participants to join the discussion briefly. (Fifteen minutes.)

XIII. The facilitator summarizes the major learnings, focusing on the following issues: (1) *individual feelings* provoked during the building phase of the activity; (2) the degree to which the activity reflects real conditions; (3) the identification of those elements of *individual* and *institutional racism* as reflected in the activity; (4) the alternatives to win-lose confrontations in the resolution of intergroup conflict.

Bridge Building:
An Intergroup Cooperation

Goals

    I. To encourage collaboration among team members.

    II. To experience the values and effects of both competition and cooperation.

Group Size

Any number of participants, divided into two groups. Multiple pairs of groups are possible.

Time Required

Approximately one and one-half hours.

Materials

    I. Two card tables placed six feet apart.

    II. A collection of miscellaneous materials, such as paper cups, tape, paper plates, crepe paper, etc., placed on the two tables.

Process

    I. The facilitator divides the participants into two groups.

    II. Each group is asked to choose a representative.

    III. Each group chooses one or two observers who will take notes during the activity and give feedback later.

    IV. Observers are briefed on what to look for during the activity: influence patterns, cooperation, work attitudes, division of labor, norms, response to time pressure, leadership styles, etc.

    V. The facilitator explains the purpose of the activity. Using only the materials available, the two groups are to build one bridge which begins on each table and spans the space between. The groups begin at separate tables and work to connect the bridge near the middle of the span. The bridge

---

Submitted by Allan R. Cohen and Herman Gadon.

should be as strong, original, and beautiful as possible. *The object of the activity is for both groups to collaborate to build the best bridge possible.* However, to duplicate usual organizational conditions, the groups can communicate only through their representatives. The representatives may meet as often as they like, during all phases of the exercise: designing the bridge, planning its construction, and building it. They may tell their groups as much or as little about the meetings as they like, and they may be as open as they like when meeting with the other representatives.

VI. A maximum of one hour is allowed for the construction of the bridge.

VII. When the bridge is completed or the time is up, the observers report to the entire group.

VIII. The facilitator leads a general discussion considering the following groups of questions:
1. What did it feel like to be a representative? What did it feel like to be a worker? How did each group feel about the other? How did members feel about the emergent leaders and their styles?
2. Did representatives try to influence their group or to represent it? Did representatives try to collaborate or compete?
3. If competition arose, from where and whom did it come? How was it initiated? What were the consequences?
4. What obvious mistakes were made in the design? Why? Were the groups creative? Why or why not?
5. Was everyone involved? Were all resources in each group used? Did everyone have a satisfying role? Did anyone want more influence on his own group than he had? Results?
6. Was there any stereotyping of the other group? Where did this come from?

IX. The facilitator refocuses the discussion toward the *implications* of this experience for improving minority-group relations.

Instrumentation in
Minority Relations

Introduction to Instruments

USING INSTRUMENTS IN LABORATORY EDUCATION*

Nonclinical measurement devices can be highly useful in a laboratory education design. They can serve to focus on particular behavioral science concepts and can provide a set of data whereby participants can explore themselves intra- and interpersonally, study group composition, and discover new behaviors in which they might consider engaging within the relative safety of the laboratory milieu. The Instrumentation section of this book is designed to provide easy access to instruments that might be incorporated into laboratory designs.

A useful style is to introduce an instrument by encouraging participants to be very open in responding to the items, to ask participants to complete the scale, to lecture on the rationale underlying the instrument, to illustrate the interpretation of the scoring by using actual staff scores for examples, and to have participants practice interpreting each other's scores (usually in helping pairs). It is helpful to follow this by posting the data to build norms for the particular laboratory and then processing the data in intensive small-group meetings that tend to focus on the personal relevance of the data at a relatively higher support level than characterizes individual interpretation. Instruments are not substitutes for experiential approaches, but they can often serve as highly effective means of focusing learning around a theoretical model.

The four basic laboratory components—intensive small groups, structured experiences, lecturettes, and instruments—can be varied almost infinitely to provide highly innovative, flexible designs to meet the learning needs of participants.

---

*This discussion is taken from J. William Pfeiffer and Richard Heslin, *Instrumentation in Human Relations Training*, La Jolla, Ca.: University Associates, 1973; and J. E. Jones and J. W. Pfeiffer, *The 1973 Annual Handbook for Group Facilitators*, La Jolla, Ca.: University Associates, 1973.

Instruments can be used in a number of ways by group facilitators. Data from inventories can be interpreted normatively or intrapersonally, but it is important that they be coordinated carefully with the goals of the training design. Some uses of instrumentation include the following:

Providing instrumented feedback to group members. Participants complete, score, and interpret their own scales. They can be asked to predict each other's scores. They can fill out scales for each other as feedback.

Manipulating group composition. For brief, experimental demonstrations of the effects of group composition, various mixes of group members can be established. Long-term groups can be built that offer the promise of beneficial outcomes. Extremes of both homogeneity and heterogeneity can be avoided.

Teaching theory of interpersonal functioning. Some brief instruments are intended primarily to introduce concepts. Participants are involved with theory by investing in an activity such as completing an inventory related to the model being explored.

Researching outcomes of training interventions. Even scales with relatively low reliability can be effective in the study of group phenomena when used with pretest or follow-up procedures.

Studying here-and-now process in groups. It is sometimes helpful to use an instrument to assist the group in diagnosing its own internal functioning. The data can be focused on what is happening and what changes are desirable.

INSTRUMENTS IN INTERGROUP AND MINORITY-GROUP RELATIONS

The four instruments included in this section are designed to help participants assess themselves and to promote discussion of race-related attitudes. They can be easily reproduced as training instruments. Each of the instruments measures an important aspect of intergroup and minority-group relations.

"The Chitlin' Test" is a "classic" instrument of unknown origin that has two major uses: (1) to teach that cultural deprivation is situation-specific—the members of the dominant majority may be ignorant of the culture of others; and (2) to motivate participants early in training to explore their attitudes about minority-group cultures.

"Three Photos" is an instrument of the projective type, in which one interprets visual stimuli according to one's own attitudes. Two important uses of this instrument are (1) to teach the concept of projection (putting oneself into one's descriptions of others), and (2) to teach group consensus seeking through discussion of participants' responses.

The "Personal Attitude Inventory" is a community survey instrument that is easily adaptable for use in laboratory education training designs. Three principal uses of the scale are suggested: (1) as a discussion starter, (2) as a survey instrument, and (3) as an intergroup value-clarification device. The instrument can be rewritten, using local issues. Responses to the individual items can be indicated by a show-of-hands procedure.

The "Equal Employment Quiz" focuses on attitudes, values, and beliefs about hiring and race relations within an organization. It can be used several ways: (1) as a survey instrument in organization assessment and diagnosis, (2) as a stimulator of problem-identification discussions, and (3) as an inventory of the beliefs that training participants hold about equal opportunity in a local setting. It can be rewritten to fit local conditions, practices, and policies. Tallies of the responses of members of identifiable subgroups, such as blacks, Chicanos, etc., can be made and recorded for discussion purposes.

DEVELOPING INSTRUMENTED TRAINING APPROACHES

The instruments in this section are offered as *examples* of what can be done to open up intergroup and minority-group relations topics and issues within training settings. The formats of these examples are varied, and users of this book are encouraged to develop comparable instruments that are relevant to the particular environments in which training and developmental activities are carried out.

It is often helpful to engage members of various client groups in the task of preparing instruments, to insure content validity and to make the "product" more credible to the training participants.

The Chitlin' Test

Part I—Multiple Choice

Circle the answer that you think is correct.

1. In the ghetto the opposite of square is . . .
   a. round.
   b. up.
   c. down.
   d. with it.

2. A "Pik" is a . . .
   a. T.V. show.
   b. comb.
   c. demonstration.
   d. policeman.

3. "Tell it . . ."
   a. as it is.
   b. how it is.
   c. like it is.
   d. straight.

4. If a man is called "chicken eater," he is . . .
   a. a cool cat.
   b. a porter.
   c. a preacher.
   d. an Uncle Tom.

5. "You got to get up early to . . ."
   a. catch worms.
   b. be healthy.
   c. fool me.
   d. be first on the street.

6. If a man is called "blood," he is . . .
   a. a prize fighter.
   b. a Mexican-American.
   c. a Black.
   d. an American Indian.

7. How long does it take to clean chitlins?

    a. 15 minutes.
    b. 24 hours.
    c. 1 week.
    d. 1 hour.

8. January 15th is important in the ghetto. Why?

    a. Martin Luther King's birthday.
    b. Booker T. Washington's birthday.
    c. Lincoln freed the slaves on this date.
    d. Texas freed its slaves on this date.

9. In the ghetto "process" refers to . . .

    a. military separation.
    b. routine of daily living.
    c. a junkie.
    d. straightened hair.

10. A "do rag" is a . . .

    a. cleaning woman's duster.
    b. dance step.
    c. sweat band.
    d. pimp's attire.

Part II—Fill-Ins

Fill in the names signified by the following initials.

1. N.A.A.C.P. _____

2. S.N.C.C. _____

3. C.O.R.E. _____

4. B.P.P. _____

5. OPERATION P.U.S.H. _____

6. S.C.L.C. _____

7. B.L.A. _____

Part III—Matching

___ 1. Edward W. Brooke

___ 2. Berry Gordy, Jr.

___ 3. Marcus Garvey

___ 4. W.E.B. DuBois

___ 5. Black Panthers

___ 6. Shirley Chisholm

___ 7. Elijah Muhammed

___ 8. Julian Bond

___ 9. Dr. Martin Luther King

___10. Malcolm X

___11. Thurgood Marshall

___12. Thomas Bradley

___13. James Brown

a. Mayor, Los Angeles, California

b. Back-to-Africa movement

c. Brooklyn Congressional representative

d. Nobel Peace Prize winner

e. U.S. Senator

f. President, Motown Records

g. U.S. Supreme Court Judge

h. founder of N.A.A.C.P.

i. assassinated black nationalist

j. "Black is beautiful"

k. Georgia State Legislator

l. soul brother #1

m. Nation of Islam

The Chitlin' Test Answer Key

Part I

1. (d)—**with it.** Term used to denote someone who is knowledgeable of events taking place.

2. (b)—**comb.** An instrument with long, widely spaced teeth which is used to comb hair. Also called an "Afro Pic."

3. (c)—**like it is.**

4. (c)—**a preacher.** Term alludes to the "free" Sunday dinners preachers obtain from church members.

5. (d)—**be first on the street.** To keep abreast of what goes on in a day one would have to be on the street early.

6. (c)—**a Black.** Used by blacks to denote one of the same roots and origin.

7. (b)—**24 hours.** To clean and soak pig intestines is a day-long process.

8. (a)—**Martin Luther King's birthday.**

9. (d)—**straightened hair.** A "process" or "processed head" is the final product when chemical preparations are applied to the hair of blacks to straighten the texture.

10. (c)—**sweat band.** A "do" is another name for a process or straightened hair. Some users of a process tie handkerchiefs or cloths around their heads to prevent perspiration from ruining their hair treatment.

Part II

1. N.A.A.C.P. **National Association for the Advancement of Colored People**

2. S.N.C.C. **Student Non-Violent Coordinating Committee**

3. C.O.R.E. **Congress of Racial Equality**

4. B.P.P. **Black Panther Party**

5. OPERATION P.U.S.H. **People United to Save Humanity**

6. S.C.L.C. **Southern Christian Leadership Conference**

7. B.L.A. **Black Liberation Army**

Part III

e	1.	Edward W. Brooke	a.	Mayor, Los Angeles, California
f	2.	Berry Gordy, Jr.	b.	Back-to-Africa Movement
b	3.	Marcus Garvey	c.	Brooklyn Congressional representative
h	4.	W.E.B. DuBois	d.	Nobel Peace Prize winner
j	5.	Black Panthers	e.	U.S. Senator
c	6.	Shirley Chisholm	f.	President, Motown Records
m	7.	Elijah Muhammed	g.	U.S. Supreme Court Judge
k	8.	Julian Bond	h.	founder of N.A.A.C.P.
d	9.	Dr. Martin Luther King	i.	assassinated black nationalist
i	10.	Malcolm X	j.	"Black is beautiful"
g	11.	Thurgood Marshall	k.	Georgia State Legislator
a	12.	Thomas Bradley	l.	soul brother #1
l	13.	James Brown	m.	Nation of Islam

Three Photos

This instrument is designed to offer you a chance to examine some of your attitudes about race and the way these feelings affect your handling of racial problems in the organization in which you work.

Directions: Please indicate on the following pages your opinion, as honestly as possible, of the statements listed beneath each picture. Rate them as follows:

1. I strongly disagree.
2. I somewhat disagree.
3. I somewhat agree.
4. I strongly agree.

Michael D. Sullivan

1. People who have children they cannot support are irresponsible.

   Strongly disagree   1   2   3   4   Strongly agree

2. Children should have the support of the government if their parents cannot support them.

   Strongly disagree   1   2   3   4   Strongly agree

3. There is no reason people have to live like this.

   Strongly disagree   1   2   3   4   Strongly agree

4. Black people are socially deprived.

   Strongly disagree   1   2   3   4   Strongly agree

5. Black people still live under economically disadvantaged conditions as they did during slavery.

   Strongly disagree   1   2   3   4   Strongly agree

The Design Element

1. The "raised fist" means violence.

   Strongly disagree   1   2   3   4   Strongly agree

2. Blacks make me angry when they do this and I see it.

   Strongly disagree   1   2   3   4   Strongly agree

3. He seems to be saying that he will fight.

   Strongly disagree   1   2   3   4   Strongly agree

4. I really don't know what this "raised fist" salute means.

   Strongly disagree   1   2   3   4   Strongly agree

5. People who resent their country should leave and go somewhere else.

   Strongly disagree   1   2   3   4   Strongly agree

6. Black people need their unity as shown by the "clenched fist."

   Strongly disagree   1   2   3   4   Strongly agree

7. The "clenched fist" is only a form of greeting and it does not bother me.

   Strongly disagree   1   2   3   4   Strongly agree

The Design Element

1. These people have denied their race.

   Strongly disagree   1   2   3   4   Strongly agree

2. The white girl most likely does not have good morals.

   Strongly disagree   1   2   3   4   Strongly agree

3. The white girl is ruining her reputation by going out with a black.

   Strongly disagree   1   2   3   4   Strongly agree

4. This couple will have a lot of trouble with society.

   Strongly disagree   1   2   3   4   Strongly agree

5. You don't marry a race, you marry an individual.

   Strongly disagree   1   2   3   4   Strongly agree

6. Black men are hung up on white women.

   Strongly disagree   1   2   3   4   Strongly agree

7. White women are the aggressors with black men.

   Strongly disagree   1   2   3   4   Strongly agree

8. There is something wrong with interracial dating.

   Strongly disagree   1   2   3   4   Strongly agree

9. The black man needs to be told he does not have the right to deal socially or sexually with white women.

   Strongly disagree   1   2   3   4   Strongle agree

10. People of different races should date only in their own race.

   Strongly disagree   1   2   3   4   Strongly agree

Personal Attitude Inventory

People in any community differ widely in their views about many issues and problems. The purpose of this inventory is to provide an opportunity for the expression of the full spectrum of opinion in the community.

Directions: Please indicate your agreement or disagreement with the statements in this inventory. Circle the number that best states your opinion:

   0 if you *strongly disagree* with the item;

   1 if you generally disagree;

   2 if you neither agree nor disagree;

   3 if you generally agree;

   4 if you *strongly agree* with the item.

There are no right or wrong answers to these items. All we want is your honest opinion.

1. In spite of all the progress in recent years, the institutions in American society are still basically racist in character.

   Strongly disagree   0   1   2   3   4   Strongly agree

2. Blacks have never had it so good; their problems of getting better jobs and getting ahead in life are no different from those of ordinary white families.

   Strongly disagree   0   1   2   3   4   Strongly agree

3. In a town like this, we all should commit ourselves to reconciliation, cooperation, mutual respect, and affection between the races as a community goal.

   Strongly disagree   0   1   2   3   4   Strongly agree

4. In a town like this, blacks and only blacks should make the decisions and take the actions that affect black people. Sympathetic whites may give financial support but the power should be in the hands of the black people in the community.

   Strongly disagree   0   1   2   3   4   Strongly agree

Prepared by Howard Baumgartel, Horace Bond, Walter H. Crockett, Roland Hurst, and Vernell Sturns.

5. The people in this town and the whole American society really owe the black people something special to make up for all the past oppression and discrimination.

Strongly disagree   0   1   2   3   4   Strongly agree

6. Interracial dating and marriage should be encouraged as a way of getting rid of racial conflict in the United States.

Strongly disagree   0   1   2   3   4   Strongly agree

7. A black action group will probably need to engage in confrontation tactics and violence from time to time in order to make real progress with the white power structure.

Strongly disagree   0   1   2   3   4   Strongly agree

8. Groups from outside this community, some with communist leanings, are using local unrest to further their own radical goals.

Strongly disagree   0   1   2   3   4   Strongly agree

9. During times of crisis, there should be severe penalties for the possession of guns outside the home by unauthorized persons.

Strongly disagree   0   1   2   3   4   Strongly agree

10. There are organized white groups in this town who are planning to "take the law into their own hands" in the event of racial strife.

Strongly disagree   0   1   2   3   4   Strongly agree

11. Most white people in a town like this feel that they have worked hard for what they have and they resent special consideration given to blacks.

Strongly disagree   0   1   2   3   4   Strongly agree

12. There are organized black groups who are planning to use violent methods to obtain social reforms in this town.

Strongly disagree   0   1   2   3   4   Strongly agree

13. The main reason that black families are crowded into substandard housing is that the whole system prevents them from getting better jobs and moving into all-white neighborhoods.

Strongly disagree   0   1   2   3   4   Strongly agree

14. Business and industry should take the lead in hiring under-qualified black people even where qualified whites are available. Only by this means can the conditions of black Americans be improved.

Strongly disagree   0   1   2   3   4   Strongly agree

15. Afro-American history should be offered as a specific course in the city's schools, and it should be required of all students.

Strongly disagree   0   1   2   3   4   Strongly agree

16. Ninety percent of all student activities in the city's high school are controlled by white middle-class students.

Strongly disagree   0   1   2   3   4   Strongly agree

17. Afro-American history should be integrated into all courses in American history offered in the city's school system.

Strongly disagree   0   1   2   3   4   Strongly agree

18. The city's high school is just not interested in helping students who are not planning to go to college.

Strongly disagree   0   1   2   3   4   Strongly agree

19. As soon as blacks move into a neighborhood, deterioration sets in and property values go down.

Strongly disagree   0   1   2   3   4   Strongly agree

20. Most whites wonder what it is that the blacks really want. Actually, all they want is what every other American wants—a chance to get some of the good things out of life.

Strongly disagree   0   1   2   3   4   Strongly agree

21. The whole welfare system, as it operates in this city and else-where, works in such a way as to hold down and subjugate black people.

Strongly disagree   0   1   2   3   4   Strongly agree

22. The real problem with the angry black youth of today is that their families and community do not control them properly.

Strongly disagree   0   1   2   3   4   Strongly agree

23. In spite of everything, the blacks have a unique problem in gaining a sense of personal self-esteem, and that is a big part of what black power is all about.

Strongly disagree   0   1   2   3   4   Strongly agree

24. People who want to protest a law that they feel is unjust should conscientiously break that law, but they should be willing to pay the penalty imposed for doing so.

Strongly disagree   0   1   2   3   4   Strongly agree

25. The real motive underlying the "law-and-order" movement in the United States is to keep blacks in their place.

Strongly disagree   0   1   2   3   4   Strongly agree

26. A town like this should have a biracial police review board to deal with allegations of discrimination and injustice in police-community relations.

Strongly disagree   0   1   2   3   4   Strongly agree

27. The way justice is administered in this county, it frequently discriminates against members of minority groups.

Strongly disagree   0   1   2   3   4   Strongly agree

28. Sometimes the courts in this county and elsewhere use the judicial system to punish political and personal nonconformity.

Strongly disagree   0   1   2   3   4   Strongly agree

29. It is an irony that low-income whites are the most anti-black when in reality they should be joining forces with low-income blacks to get a better share of the good things in American life.

Strongly disagree   0   1   2   3   4   Strongly agree

30. A lot of our problems result from the fact that the community and the courts have become much too permissive in handling militancy and delinquency.

Strongly disagree   0   1   2   3   4   Strongly agree

31. *Complete the following sentence:* The biggest obstacle to improving race relations in this town and in this county is . . .

32. *Complete the following sentence:* The thing I fear the most about the current situation in this town is . . .

Several items in this inventory were adapted from "M-Scale" by James H. Morrison, 9804 Hadley, Overland Park, Kansas 66212, copyright J. H. Morrison, 1968 and 1969. Permission must be obtained from Mr. Morrison before reproducing the "Personal Attitude Inventory."

Equal Employment Quiz

Instructions: This is a survey of your attitudes about equal opportunity in this organization. Respond to each item according to your own feelings and beliefs, marking each either "true" or "false." This quiz is for discussion purposes only and will *not* be graded or reviewed by anyone.

True   **False**

1. The equal-opportunity program was started to wipe out discrimination in Federal employment.

2. Complaints of discrimination based on race or religion should be handled by the organization's personnel officer.

3. The organization has established quotas for hiring black employees.

4. An equal-employment-opportunity program applies to American Indians and Puerto Ricans as well as to blacks.

5. It would be proper, in some communities, to assign only whites to work in white areas and only blacks to work in black areas.

6. Full compliance with the equal-employment-opportunity program requires that the organization relax character and suitability standards.

7. Proportionately, about as many blacks as whites pass civil service exams.

8. The organization's merit system is being circumvented in order to fully implement this program.

9. Employee groups and unions may exclude minority groups in order to represent fairly the majority of employees.

True   **False**

_____   _____   10. The supervisor's responsibility, under this program, is to change subordinates' attitudes on racial matters whenever necessary.

_____   _____   11. The organization makes extra efforts to ensure that blacks are aware of our job opportunities.

_____   _____   12. The performance of white and black employees is judged by the same standards.

_____   _____   13. Official complaints of discrimination based on race have usually been resolved in favor of the complainant.

_____   _____   14. Settling complaints of racial discrimination is the most important aspect of this program.

_____   _____   15. When a supervisor hears someone allege discrimination, he should immediately turn the problem over to higher management.

_____   _____   16. Special efforts should be made to ensure that minority-group employees are fully utilized.

_____   _____   17. Special recruitment efforts are underway to recruit blacks, but it is better if such efforts are not generally known to employees.

_____   _____   18. Organizational representatives should visit black high schools even though most recruitment efforts are directed toward college graduates.

_____   _____   19. Organizational representatives should avoid contacts with local black "action groups" since such contacts could result in unfavorable publicity.

_____   _____   20. An employee who joins the NAACP effort directed toward nondiscrimination in education should be advised to drop such activity because adverse publicity may embarrass the organization or may otherwise reduce the employee's effectiveness on the job.

Resources

A Selected Bibliography

Books

Allen, V. L. (Ed.). *Psychological factors in poverty*. Chicago: Markham, 1970.

Baldwin, J. *Notes of a native son*. New York: Bantam, 1964.

Bloom, L. *The social psychology of race relations*. Cambridge, Mass.: Schenkman, 1972.

Ford, D. L., Jr. (Ed.). *Readings in minority-group relations*. La Jolla, Ca.: University Associates, 1975.

Fromkin, H. L., & Sherwood, J. J. (Eds.). *Integrating the organization: A social psychological analysis*. New York: Free Press, 1974.

Ginzberg, E. (Ed.). *The negro challenge to the business community*. New York: McGraw-Hill, 1964.

Grier, W. H., & Cobbs, P. M. *Black rage*. New York: Basic Books, 1968.

Griffin, J. H. *Black like me*. New York: New American Library, 1961.

Halpern, F. *Survival: Black and white*. Elmsford, N.Y.: Pergamon Press, 1973.

Jones, J. M. *Prejudice and racism*. Reading, Mass.: Addison-Wesley, 1972.

King, M. L., Jr. *Why we can't wait*. New York: American Library, 1963.

Mead, M., & Baldwin, J. *A rap on race*. New York: J. P. Lippincott, 1971.

Northrup, H. R., Rowan, R. L., et. al. *Negro employment in basic industry: A study of racial policies in six industries*. Philadelphia: University of Pennsylvania Press, 1970.

Powell, R. M. *Race, religion, and the promotion of the American executive*. Columbus: Ohio State University, College of Administrative Science, 1969.

Purcell, T. V., & Cavanaugh, G. *Blacks in the industrial world: Issues for the manager.* New York: Free Press, 1972.

Schuman, H., & Hatchett, S. *Black racial attitudes: Trends and complexities.* Ann Arbor, Mich.: Institute for Social Research, 1974.

Journals/Magazines

A "hire blacks" drive backfires. *Business Week,* April 1972, pp. 23-24.

Aiken, W. The black experience in large public accounting firms. *Journal of Accountancy,* August 1972, pp. 60-63.

Aldrich, H. E. Employment opportunities for blacks in the black ghetto: The role of the white-owned businesses. *American Journal of Sociology,* 1973, *78*(6), 1403-1425.

Ash, P. Job satisfaction differences among women of different ethnic groups. *Journal of Vocational Behavior,* 1972, *2*(4), 495-507.

Bass, A. R., & Turner, J. N. Ethnic group differences in relationships among criteria of job performance. *Journal of Applied Psychology,* 1973, *57*(2), 101-109.

Beatty, R. W. Blacks as supervisors: A study of training, job performance, and employers' expectations. *Academy of Management Journal,* 1973, *16*(2), 196-206.

Bloom, R., & Barry, J. R. Determinants of work attitudes among Negroes. *Journal of Applied Psychology,* 1967, *51*(31), 291-294.

Borus, J. F., et al. Racial perceptions in the army: An approach. *American Journal of Psychiatry,* 1972, *128*(11), 1369-1374.

Brigham, J. Ethnic stereotypes. *Psychological Bulletin,* 1971, *76*(1), 15-38.

Clark, K. B. No gimmicks, please, whitey. *Training in Business and Industry,* November 1968, pp. 27-30.

Curl, D. H. A.V. training—New films about hard-core unemployment solutions. *Training in Business and Industry,* February 1969, pp. 16-20.

Delbecq, A. L., & Kaplan, S. J. The myth of the indigenous community leader. *Academy of Management Journal,* 1968, *11,* 11-25.

Domm, D. R., & Stafford, J. E. Assimilating blacks into the organization. *California Management Review,* 1972, *15*(1), 46-51.

Feldman, J. M. Race, employment, and the evaluation of work. *Journal of Applied Psychology,* 1973, *58*(1), 10-15.

Ferman, L. Guidelines for affirmative action in equal employment opportunity. *The Negro and Equal Employment Opportunity: A Review of Management Experiences in Twenty Companies,* 1966, pp. 128-151.

Fredrichs, A. H. Relationship of self-esteem of the disadvantaged to school success. *Journal of Negro Education,* 1970, *39,* 117-120.

Fromkin, H. L., Klimoski, R. J., & Flanagan, M. F. Race and competence as determinants of acceptance of newcomers in success and failure work groups. *Organizational Behavior and Human Performance,* 1972, *7*(1), 25-42.

Greenhaus, J. H., & Gavin, J. F. The relationship between expectancies and job behavior for white and black employees. *Personnel Psychology,* 1972, *25,* 449-455.

Hill, W., & Fox, W. M. Black and white Marine squad leaders' perceptions of racially mixed squads. *Academy of Management Journal,* 1973, *16*(4), 680-686.

Holsendolph, E. Black executives in a nearly all-white world. *Fortune,* September 1972.

Howard, D. H. An exploratory study of attitudes of Negro professionals toward competition with whites. *Social Forces,* 1966, *45*(1), 20-27.

Jones, E. W. What it's like to be a black manager. *Harvard Business Review,* July-August 1973, pp. 108-116.

Katz, I., & Cohen, M. The effects of training Negroes upon cooperative problem solving in biracial teams. *Journal of Abnormal and Social Psychology,* 1962, *64*(5), 319-325.

Katz, I., Goldston, J., & Benjamin, L. Behavior and productivity in bi-racial work groups. *Human Relations,* 1958, *11,* 123-141.

Kirchner, W., & Lucas, J. Some research on motivating the hard-core. *Training in Business and Industry,* 1971, *8,* 30-31.

Lakin, M., & Schiffman, H. Sensitivity training and interracial communication. *Training News,* 1966, *10,* 2-4.

London, J., & Hammett, R. Impact of company policy upon discrimination. *Sociology and Social Research,* 1954, *39,* 88-91.

Muir, D. E. The first years of desegregation. *Social Forces,* 1971, *49*(3), 371-378.

Nason, R. W. The dilemma of black mobility in management. *Business Horizons,* August 1972, pp. 57-68.

Palmer, E. H. Finding and keeping minority group managers. *Personnel,* January-February 1969, pp. 13-17.

Pati, G. C., & Fahey, P. E. Affirmative action program: Its realities and challenges. *Labor Law Journal,* June 1973, *24*(6), 351-361.

Petroni, F. "Uncle Toms": White stereotypes in the black movement. *Human Organization,* 1970, *29*(4), 260-266.

Purcell, T., & Cavanagh, G. Making minority policies effective. R. Clark (Ed.), *Contact Magazine,* 1973, *3*, 46-49.

Richards, S. A., & Jaffee, C. L. Blacks supervising whites: A study of interracial difficulties in working together in a simulated organization. *Journal of Applied Psychology,* 1972, *56*(3), 234-240.

Seligman, D. How equal opportunity turned into employment quotas. *Business Horizons,* August 1972, pp. 57-68.

Slocum, J. W., Jr., & Strauser, R. H. Racial differences in job attitudes. *Journal of Applied Psychology,* 1972, *56*(1), 28-32.

Taylor, S. The black executive and the corporation—a difficult fit. *MBA,* January 1972.

Taylor, S. Room at the top? Not for blacks. *New York Times,* January 14, 1973.

Travaglio, R., Sloan, D., & Walker, J. W. Difficulties of black supervisors. *Training and Development Journal,* February 1971, pp. 33-34.

Triandis, H. C., & Malpass, R. S. Studies of black and white interaction in job settings. *Journal of Applied Social Psychology,* 1971, *1*, 101-117.

Unterman, I. Minority group managers: What's wrong with opportunities in business? *Personnel,* 1971.

Watson, P. The racial gap. *Psychology Today,* September 1972.

What business can do for the Negro. *Nation's Business,* October 1967, pp. 67-70.

Woodall, T. E. From crisis to collaboration: Thoughts on the use of laboratory method in resolving black-white issues. *Social Change,* 1971, *1*, 1-3.

Zuel, C., & Humphrey, C. The integration of black residents in suburban neighborhoods. *Social Problems,* Spring 1971, *18*, 462-474.

A List of Related Cases*

(6G129) The Well-Run Oil Company
Hiring additional Negro employees. Group of organized Negro ministers threaten economic boycott.

(9G180) Harper's Laundry, Inc.
Problems of adverse internal situations and external environments.

(9G181) Polly Prim Associates, Inc.
Problems of adverse internal situations and external environments.

(12G97) F. Johnson's Food Store
Problems of pricing, misrepresentation of goods, and racial integration. Ethical issues of white owners and Negro clientele.

(12G104) Reflections on Housing the Poor
Cause and effect of substandard urban housing; public housing program.

(13G1) The Stonetown Real Estate Corporation
Financial support for real estate operations in predominantly Negro area and programs for social change.

(13G27) Eastern Gas and Fuel Associates
Corporate planning of new communities and ghetto rehabilitation.

(13G43) Isaac Steinhart
Efforts of a white educator to institute business courses for blacks in the ghetto.

(13G49) Potter Manufacturing Company
Use of tests in hiring Negroes.

(13G51) Crawford Manufacturing Company (A)
Planning problems, emphasizing race relations and ghetto problems.

(13G52) Crawford Manufacturing Company (B)
Personnel policies, emphasizing race relations and ghetto problems.

(13G53) Continental Baking Company
A Negro boycott against a Wonder Bread bakery.

(13G60) The Kennedy Proposal
Legislation about building low-rent housing in ghetto areas.

---

*These cases are indexed under Black Business and Racial Problems in *Selected Cases in Business Administration, Volumes XI-XIII with Cumulative Index—Volumes I-XIII*, (Intercollegiate Bibliography), 1970.

(13G113) First Pennsylvania Banking and Trust Company (A)
Adoption of policy for increasing Negro participation in Philadelphia's business community.

(13G114) First Pennsylvania Banking and Trust Company (B)
Policy in action.

(13G115) First Pennsylvania Banking and Trust Company (C)
Difficulties in development.

(13G212) Bergen County Chamber of Commerce (A)
Bus service for low-skilled workers from depressed urban areas to suburban industrial plants.

(13G225) The Bank of America-CORE Dispute on Equal Employment Opportunity
Discrimination in hiring policies—goals and strategies; other institutions involved.

(13G250) Consolidated Edison Company of New York (B)
Company relations with the black community.

(13G298) Duffield Dairy Company (A)
Efforts to increase number of minority-group employees.

(13G300) The Hough Development Corporation—Introduction
Life in ghetto from point of view of ghetto resident.

(13G301) The Hough Development Corporation (A)
Federally financed business development organization in black ghetto.

(13G302) The Hough Development Corporation (B)
Personal life and objectives of black leader. Organizational problems of president of black business development group.

(13G303) The Hough Development Corporation (C)
Role of white in black business development organization.

(13G304) The Hough Development Corporation (D)
Role of black community leader in business entrepreneurship group. Personal objectives.

(13G305) The Hough Development Corporation (E)
Black leader looks at his role and discusses hopes for black community.

(13G306) The Hough Development Corporation (F)
Role of management consulting firm in assistant black minority business.

(13G307) The Hough Development Corporation (G)
Role of white outside consultant in black development organization.

(13G312) **Chrysler Corporation**
Company efforts to hire and train the culturally disadvantaged unemployed.

(13G316) **The New Yorker Magazine (N)**
Decision about accepting advertising from the South African Government Tourist Office. Racial equality and diplomatic relations.

(13G331) **Jackson Auto**
Successful noncolor-based marketing strategy vs. black political goals and moral principles.

(13G344) **Avco Corporation**
Establishing new division in ghetto area; hiring and training program.

(13G361) **Alabama Textile Products Corporation**
Integration of textile mill in Alabama.

(DC3H2) **James Tanner, (Parts A-D)**
VISTA volunteer's reactions to racial discrimination in employment agency.

(7H81) **Prince Candy Company**
Labor unionization of paternalistic company—changing social values, worker loyalties, and alleged racial discrimination.

(9H4) **National Manufacturing Corporation**
Recruiting qualified Negro personnel for technical and craftsman positions in Southern firm.

(9H8) **Southern Manufacturing Corporation**
Employee motivation and racial problems in the South.

(9H59) **The J. C. Carter Company**
Compensating, training, and supervising Negro in typical, small paternalistic business in the South.

(9H61) **A Negro Executive**
Experiences of a Negro in achieving business success.

(10H15) **Warwick Electronics, Inc.**
Plant location and equal-employment-opportunity policy.

(10H40) **Knowles Realty Company and the North Shore Summer Project**
Problems of showing and selling a house to a Negro customer.

(11H53) **Nicholson Products Rhodesia Pvt., Ltd.**
Human problems of building a racially integrated subsidiary in Rhodesia.

(11H67) **A Case of Discrimination?**
Personnel department vs. supervisors on equal opportunity employment.

(12H4) Ralfon Electronics Company

Discharged Negro employee charges racial discrimination.

(12H5) Vance-Wheeler Corporation

Negro employee charges company with discrimination for not promoting him to a supervisory position.

(12H65) Border State Bus Company (A)

Company faced with threat of violence, wildcat strike, and economic boycott because of one of its employees (Acting Grand Dragon of Ku Klux Klan).

(12H66) Border State Bus Company (B)

Company's discharge of employee and union's demand for arbitration.

(12H67) Border State Bus Company (C)

Summarizes the arbitrator's ruling.

(12H68) Eastman Kodak and FIGHT

Hiring and training of hard-core unemployed.

(13H15) Herren's

Racial integration of restaurant.

(13H22) Leb's

Racial integration of restaurant—civil rights demonstrators and their opponents.

(13H31) Rush at Digma Si

Reaction of fraternity members to anonymous veto of a Negro pledge candidate.

(9M27) Alonto Coke & Coal Company (A)

Small new firm and marketing policy—minority group salesman.

(11M72) Rogevi Trading

Conversion of appliance business into discount house operation—Chinese business practices.

(13M17) Carnham & Loy

Racially integrated advertising for different products and different types of consumers.

(14G52) Cooper Realty Co.—S. Block, Texas Christian Univ.

Investment problems of a white property owner in a minority group area. Consider best financial course of action and social responsibility.

(15G53) Centaur Shop—I. H. Harrison, Texas Christian Univ.

Black entrepreneur in black neighborhood faces problems of financing, selling, and purchasing.

(15G54) Multifab Manufacturing Co.—L. R. Trueblood, Univ. of Tulsa

Bi-racial ownership, management, and employees of enterprise. Huge deficits incurred in two years of operation.

(14G62) **Apex Oil Co.**—H. G. Hicks & G. E. Popp, Louisiana State Univ.
Problems of recruiting minority engineering personnel, salary increases, and
use of technicians.

(14G73) **Providing Housing for Inner-City Families**—F. E. Case, Univ.
of California, Los Angeles
After deciding to make loans in the inner city, a large bank runs into difficulties
which lead to new lending policies and programs.

Racial Conflict and Negotiations: Perspectives and First Case Studies
Edited by W. Ellison Chalmers and Gerald W. Cormick. February 1971. 252
pages. $10.00 (cloth) $3.50 (paper). The Institute of Labor and Industrial Relations, Publications Office: P.O. Box B-1, Ann Arbor, Michigan 48106.

Media Sources

Films

In the Company of Men (52 minutes, black and white, 1969). Produced and directed by William Greaves. Available from William Greaves Productions, 254 West 54th Street, New York, New York 10019.

In this remarkable documentary, we witness the use of techniques of sensitivity training and role playing in building bridges of communication between whites in supervisory positions and blacks who have been labeled hard-core unemployable. The setting is a Southern automobile factory that needs workers. Under a psychodramatist's guidance, the white foremen try to put themselves in the black men's shoes in an attempt to understand black militancy against the establishment. In group sessions with a black psychiatrist, the blacks—all potential new employees—act out and talk about the frustrating incidents that embittered them.

When the two groups are brought together, the film's basic message is made clear. Teaching white foremen to be tolerant and teaching black workers to have proper work attitudes is a dead end: the only realistic solution is a program that will enhance two-way communication, rapport, mutual understanding, and respect. A true documentary made without professional actors or a script, this film contains much emotionally charged material. Despite its length, it manages to keep one's attention fixed on the proceedings.

The film would be useful for training supervisory personnel in mental hospitals and community mental health services, and will be of special interest to those involved in sensitivity training, psychodrama, group psychotherapy, and encounter groups. *In the Company of Men* has won six film-festival awards for its candid and uninhibited approach to an especially nettlesome problem, and is well worth the attention of all who work in the behavioral sciences.

The Way Out (45 minutes, 16mm color film). Available from Instructional Dynamics Incorporated, 166 E. Superior Street, Chicago, Illinois 60611, (312) 943-1200.

The Way Out provides a close look at the backgrounds and urban environments of four ethnic groups. This incisive film shows conditions of blacks, Spanish-speaking residents, American Indians, and white Appalachians, focusing on the urban environments in which many are now forced to live. Members of each group speak about factors that keep them in conditions of unemployment and poverty.

At the end of the four presentations, two clips add an extended dimension to *The Way Out*. One shows a white supervisor and a black worker who have come to a fairly successful relationship. The other depicts two white workers reacting to the thought of blacks working in their plant, with their hostile attitudes quickly coming to the surface.

I'm Not Too Proud Anymore (20 minutes, 16mm color film). Available from Instructional Dynamics Incorporated, 166 E. Superior Street, Chicago, Illinois 60611, (312) 943-1200.

A white Appalachian who lived and worked in Chicago for fifteen years makes an impassioned plea for help on behalf of other Appalachians and disadvantaged people of all races.

Chuck Geary tells how he came to Chicago from Kentucky and worked as a day laborer for 40 cents an hour. "I came looking for gold . . . I found tin." Geary speaks, emotionally and with some anger, of the plight of the white Appalachian in the city, and says he speaks also for the black and Puerto Rican poor. They want to work, but are denied a chance.

Transparencies

Hidden Communication Barriers (15 transparencies). Available from Lansford Publishing Company, P.O. Box 8711, San Jose, California 95155, (408) 287-3105. WR301T.

Describes critical ethnic, ghetto, and cross-cultural protective mechanisms often ignored. Invites study of specific incidents and styles that needlessly frustrate mutual goals.

Cassettes/Slides

The Feminist Movement (2 cassettes, supplementary materials). Available from Lansford Publishing Company, P.O. Box 8711, San Jose, California 95155, (408) 287-3105. SHA401C.

The lectures cover the development of the Women's Lib Movement: changing roles between male and female, trends in feminine discrimination, and new directions for modern women. Each is 20 to 30 minutes in length. Prepared by Jane Havilla, Gavilan College, Gilroy, California.

A Comparative Analysis of Organizational and Community Change Methods and Their Implications for the Black Community. Warrington S. Parker, Program Associate, Institute for Social Research, University of Michigan. Available from *Development Digest,* Published by CREDR Corporation, P.O. Box 49938, Los Angeles, California 90049. T309.

Compares and contrasts models for community change that have been initiated in the past by both external forces and internal leaders. Describes similarities and differences among methods of change in the community and the organization. Conducts a workshop with participants on specific change problems in their communities and organizations. Presents an approach for evaluating the results of a prospective change program before initiating it.

Management Workshop for Supervisors of Minority Groups. Available from Instructional Dynamics Incorporated, 166 E. Superior Street, Chicago, Illinois 60611, (312) 943-1200. Catalog No. 202—Management Workshop.

A successfully proven, widely used training experience for those responsible for supervision of minority-group employees.

Clear step-by-step instructions permit leadership by persons without prior experience. Participants see things as a new employee would, and through exercises that apply problem-solving skills to specific situations, they learn to cope constructively with attitudes of prejudice.

Instructor's manual, tape lecture, and enough exercise materials for two participants. Exercise materials consist of face masks, exercise envelopes, supplemental supervisor's notebook, and prismatic glasses.

Additional sets of participants' exercise materials (for 2) are available.

Sources for Reference Material

Afram Associates, Inc.
68–72 East 131st Street
Harlem, New York 10037
(212) 690-7010

Anti-Defamation League of B'nai B'rith
315 Lexington Avenue
New York, New York 10016

Committee for One Society
40 North Ashard Avenue
Chicago, Illinois
(312) 829-1272
Request: *Inventory of Racism: How to Look for Institutional Racism.*
[*Working Paper*] #1B

Detroit Industrial Mission
13826 West McNichols
Detroit, Michigan 48221
(313) 341-4728

Ecumenical Associates
Suite 804
Michigan National Tower
Lansing, Michigan 48933

New Detroit, Inc.
Speakers Bureau
1515 Detroit Bank and Trust Building
Detroit, Michigan 48226
(313) 961-9160

Contributors

Thomas Azumbrado
Office of Intergroup Education
Office of Instructional Services
Board of Education of the City of New York
110 Livingston Street
Brooklyn, New York 11201

Howard Baumgartel
Department of Psychology
University of Kansas
Lawrence, Kansas 66044

Robert Beneckson
Associate Group Facilitator
Cultural and Human Interaction Center
Florida International University
Trailer M1A
Tamiami Trail
Miami, Florida 33144

Horace Bond
Speech Department
University of Minnesota
Minneapolis, Minnesota 55455

Peter S. Caffentzis
Director
Research & Development
New York City Police Academy
34–53 24th Street
Long Island City, New York 11106

Eugene A. Cincotta
TRW Systems Group
One Space Park
Redondo Beach, California 90278

Allan R. Cohen
Associate Professor of Administration
Whittemore School of Business and Economics
University of New Hampshire
Durham, New Hampshire 03824

Walter H. Crockett
Department of Psychology
University of Kansas
Lawrence, Kansas 66044

Don M. Dawson
Indianapolis Area Coordinator
Involvement Corps
222 E. Ohio, Room 406
Indianapolis, Indiana 46204

John Denham
1500 Massachusetts Avenue, N.W.
Suite 325
Washington, D.C. 20005

Marvin Dunn
Associate Professor of Psychology and Director
Cultural and Human Interaction Center
Florida International University
Trailer M1A
Tamiami Trail
Miami, Florida 33144

Susan Ells
Senior Equal Opportunity Administrator
Polaroid Corporation
565 Technology Square
Cambridge, Massachusetts 02139

Arthur M. Freedman
Region 2 Training and Development Director
Illinois Department of Mental Health
160 North LaSalle Street
Chicago, Illinois 60601

Herman Gadon
Professor of Management
Whittemore School of Business and Economics
University of New Hampshire
Durham, New Hampshire 03824

Donald S. Goldman
Director, Industrial Relations
TRW Data Systems
12911 Simms Avenue
Hawthorne, California 90250

Miguel Gonzalez-Pando
Group Facilitator
Cultural and Human Interaction Center
Florida International University
Trailer M1A
Tamiami Trail
Miami, Florida 33144

Dean A. Holt
National Drug Abuse Training Center
1500 Wilson Boulevard
Rosslyn Station, Virginia 22209

Roland Hurst
Civil Engineering Department
University of Kansas
Lawrence, Kansas 66044

Ruth G. King
Associate Professor
Department of Human Ecological Systems and Services
School of Graduate Studies
Federal City College
724 9th Street, N.W. (Room 523)
Washington, D.C. 20001

Jerry Klein
formerly with McBer and Company
675 Massachusetts Avenue
Cambridge, Massachusetts 02139

David A. Landy
Apartment 7
77 South Street
Freehold, New Jersey 07728

Bertram M. Lee
President
Lee-Grigsby Associates, Inc.
15 Broad Street
Boston, Massachusetts 02109

Cyril R. Mill,
Program Director for Consultation
NTL Institute for Applied Behavioral Science
Box 9155
Rosslyn Station, Virginia 22209

Jane Moosbruker
Group and Organizational Consultant
Lecturer, Harvard University School of Dental Medicine
1039 Massachusetts Avenue
Cambridge, Massachusetts 02138

Jerry Perlmutter
George Williams College
555 Thirty-First Street
Downers Grove, Illinois 60515

Tom Puroff
Group Facilitator
Cultural and Human Interaction Center
Florida International University
Trailer M1A
Tamiami Trail
Miami, Florida 33144

James E. Richard
Executive Associate
Effectiveness Training Associates of New England
45 Chiltern Road
Weston, Massachusetts 02193

Warren H. Schmidt
Senior Lecturer
Graduate School of Management
University of California
Los Angeles, California 90024

Gail Silverman
Consultant to Organizations
4510 Adams Avenue
Miami Beach, Florida 33140

Robert Solomon
Group Facilitator
Cultural and Human Interaction Center
Florida International University
Trailer M1A
Tamiami Trail
Miami, Florida 33144

Vernell Sturns
Assistant City Manager
Fort Worth, Texas 76101

Maxine Thornton-Denham
560 N. Street, S.W.
Apartment N-704
Washington, D.C. 20024

Thomas E. Woodall
Planning Specialist
Human Resource Development Foundation
Route 8
Box 58-A
Morgantown, West Virginia 26505